KU-403-678

COLLINS GEM

DICTIONARY OF
ABBREVIATIONS

COLLINS GEM

DICTIONARY OF ABBREVIATIONS

Compiled by
Nancy Marshall

Collins
London & Glasgow

General Editor
W. T. McLeod

First Published 1980
© 1980 William Collins Sons & Co. Ltd.
ISBN 0 00 458324 8
Printed in Great Britain by
William Collins Sons & Co. Ltd.

Abbreviations

Aeron., Aeronautics	*L.*, Latin
Astron., Astronautics	*Math.*, Mathematics
(Aust.), Australia	*Met.*, Meteorology
Bib., Bible	*Mil.*, Military
(Can.), Canada	*Mus.*, Music
Chem., Chemistry	*Naut.*, Nautical
Cin., Cinema	(NZ), New Zealand
DP., Data Processing	*Obs.*, Obsolete
Elec., Electrical	*Phot.*, Photography
Fin., Finance	*Phys.*, Physics
Fr., French	*Psychol.*, Psychology
Gael., Gaelic	*Ptg.*, Printing
It., Italian	*Russ.*, Russian
IVR, International	(SAfr), South Africa
Vehicle Registration	(US), United States

Pronunciation Key

a	as in *fat*	o	as in *pot*	yoo	as in *cure*
ā	as in *date*	ō	as in *tone*	u	as in *cut*
ä	as in *car*	ô	as in *law*	ʉ	as in *fur*
e	as in *ten*	ōō	as in *tool*	ə	as in *agent*
ē	as in *meet*	ōō	as in *pull*	sh	as in *dash*
i	as in *hit*	yōō	as in *few*	ŋ	as in *ring*
ī	as in *bite*				

Notes to the User

1. Entries are set out in alphabetical order, but where
   two or more abbreviations consist of the same letters,
   they are set out as in the following example:

   CD **1.** Canadian Forces Decoration **2.**
   Chancery Division **3.** Civil Defence **4.**
   contagious disease **5.** Corps Diplomatique
   C/D **1.** Certificate of Deposit **2.**
   Customs Declaration
   Cd *Chem.* cadmium
   cd candela
   cd. **1.** cord **2.** could
   c.d. cash discount
   c/d carried down

2. Definitions within entries follow alphabetical order
   (see above example).

3. In the interests of economy, it has not been possible
   to include all the variations of capitals or lower case,
   and punctuated or unpunctuated entries. Generally,
   the unpunctuated version with capitals is given, but
   this by no means suggests that it is the only version
   in use.

4. Definitions may be supplemented by a field label, *eg*
   Chem., *IVR*, *Math.*, or a country of use, *eg* (Aust.),
   (Can.).

NANCY MARSHALL

A

A **1.** Absolute **2.** Academician
3. Academy **4.** Acting **5.** Adjutant
6. Admiral **7.** Adult **8.** Advanced
9. alcohol **10.** alto **11.** Amateur
12. America(n) **13.** ampere
14. Ångström **15.** anode **16.** answer
17. April **18.** *Math.* area **19.** *Chem.*
argon **20.** Artillery **21.** Associate
22. atomic weight **23.** *IVR* Austria

Å Ångström unit

a **1.** acceleration **2.** acre **3.** are (unit of measure)

a. **1.** about **2.** accepted **3.** acid
4. active **5.** actual **6.** address
7. adjective **8.** age **9.** alto **10.** ampere
11. *anno* (*L.* year) **12.** anode
13. anonymous **14.** answer **15.** *ante* (*L.* before) **16.** *aqua* (*L.* water) **17.** area
18. arrive

A1 first class

AA **1.** Achievement Age **2.** Advertisers' Association **3.** Air Attaché **4.** Alcoholics Anonymous **5.** Anglers' Association
6. anti-aircraft **7.** Architectural Association **8.** Associate in Accounting
9. Associate in Agriculture **10.** Associate

in Arts **11.** Augustinians of the
Assumption **12.** Automobile Association
AAA **1.** Agricultural Adjustment
Administration (US) **2.** Amateur Athletic
Association **3.** American Accounting
Association **4.** American Automobile
Association **5.** anti-aircraft artillery
6. Australian Automobile Association
AAAA **1.** Amateur Athletic Association of
America **2.** American Association of
Advertising Agencies **3.** Australian
Association of Advertising Agencies
AAAL American Academy of Arts and
Letters
AAAS **1.** American Academy of Arts and
Sciences **2.** American Association for the
Advancement of Science **3.** Associate of
the American Antiquarian Society
AAB **1.** American Association of
Bioanalysts **2.** Association of Applied
Biologists
AABL Associated Australian Banks in
London
AABM Australian Association of British
Manufacturers
AAC **1.** Agricultural Advisory Council
2. Amateur Athletic Club **3.** *anno ante
Christum* (*L.* in the year before Christ)
4. Army Air Corps **5.** automatic amplitude
control

AACCA Associate of the Association of
Certified and Corporate Accountants
AACE American Association of Cost
Engineers
AACL Association of American
Correspondents in London
AACP Anglo-American Council on
Productivity
AACR American Association for Cancer
Research
AACS Airways and Air Communications
Service (US)
AADC Air Aide-de-Camp
AAE 1. American Association of
Engineers 2. Association for Adult
Education
AAEC Australian Atomic Energy
Commission
AAEE 1. Aircraft and Armament
Experimental Establishment 2. American
Association of Electrical Engineers
AAeE Associate in Aeronautical
Engineering
AAF Army Air Force (US)
AAFA Anglo-American Families
Association
AAFCE Allied Air Forces Central Europe
AAFIS Army and Air Force Intelligence
Staff

AAFNE   Allied Air Forces Northern Europe

AAFSE   Allied Air Forces Southern Europe

AAFSS   Advanced Aerial Fire Support System

AAG   **1.** Assistant Adjutant-General **2.** Association of American Geographers

AAHE   American Association for Higher Education

AAI   **1.** Architectural Association of Ireland **2.** Associate of the Chartered Auctioneers' and Estate Agents' Institute **3.** Association of Art Institutions

AAIA   **1.** Associate of the Association of International Accountants **2.** Associate of the Australian Institute of Advertising

AAII   Associate of the Australian Insurance Institute

AAL   **1.** Academy of Art and Literature **2.** Association of Assistant Librarians

AALL   American Association for Labor Legislation

AALPA   Associate of the Incorporated Society of Auctioneers and Landed Property Agents

AAM   **1.** air-to-air missile **2.** Anti-Apartheid Movement **3.** Association of Assistant Mistresses

AAMC   **1.** Association of American

Medical Colleges **2.** Australian Army
Medical Corps

AANA Australian Association of National
Advertisers

A & A additions and amendments

A & M **1.** Agricultural and Mechanical
2. *Hymns* Ancient and Modern

A & N Army and Navy

A & R Artist and Repertoire

A & SH Argyll and Sutherland
Highlanders

AAP Australian Associated Press

AAPA Advertising Agency Production
Association

AAPC All African Peoples' Conference

AAPHI Associate of the Association of
Public Health Inspectors

AAPO All African Peoples' Organization

AAPS American Association for the
Promotion of Science

AAPSS American Academy of Political
and Social Science

AAPSW Associate of the Association of
Psychiatric Social Workers

AAPT American Association of Physics
Teachers

AAQMG Assistant Adjutant and
Quartermaster General

a.a.r. **1.** against all risks **2.** average
annual rainfall

AAS 1. *Academiae Americanae Socius* (*L.* Fellow of the American Academy of Arts and Sciences) 2. American Academy of Arts and Sciences 3. American Antiquarian Society 4. American Astronautical Society 5. American Astronomical Society 6. Associate in Applied Science 7. Association of Architects and Surveyors 8. Australian Academy of Science 9. Auxiliary Ambulance Service

AASA Associate of the Australian Society of Accountants

AASE Australian Associated Stock Exchanges

AASF Advanced Air Striking Force

AASS *Americanae Antiquarianae Societatis Socius* (*L.* Associate of the American Antiquarian Society)

AATA Anglo-American Tourist Association

AATUF All-African Trade Union Federation

AAU Amateur Athletic Union

AAUN American *or* Australian Association for the United Nations

AAUP American Association of University Professors

AAUQ Associate in Accountancy, University of Queensland

AAUW   American Association of University Women

AB   **1.** able-bodied seaman   **2.** *Artium Baccalaureus* (*L.* Bachelor of Arts)

Ab   *Chem.* alabamine

ab.   about

ABA   **1.** Amateur Boxing Association   **2.** American Bankers' Association   **3.** American Bar Association   **4.** American Booksellers' Association   **5.** Antiquarian Booksellers' Association   **6.** Associate of the British Archaeological Association   **7.** Association of British Archaeologists

ABAA   **1.** Antiquarian Booksellers' Association of America   **2.** Associate of the British Association of Accountants and Auditors

ABAC   Association of British Aero Clubs and Centres

ABAFA   Association of British Adoption and Fostering Agencies

ABAI   Amateur Basketball Association of Ireland

ABAS   Amateur Basketball Association of Scotland

Abb.   **1.** Abbess   **2.** Abbey   **3.** Abbot

ABBA   Amateur Basket Ball Association

abbr., abbrev.   **1.** abbreviated   **2.** abbreviation

ABC   **1.** Advance Booking Charter

2. American Broadcasting Company
3. Associated British Cinemas **4.** Audit
Bureau of Circulations **5.** Australian
Broadcasting Commission **6.** automatic
binary computer

ABCA Army Bureau of Current Affairs

ABCB Association of Birmingham
Clearing Banks

ABCC 1. Association of British Chambers
of Commerce **2.** Association of British
Correspondence Colleges

ABCM Associate of the Bandsman's
College of Music

ABD Association of British Detectives

abd. 1. abdicated **2.** abridged

ABF 1. Actors' Benevolent Fund
2. Associated British Foods

ABFM American Board of Foreign
Missions

ABH alpha-benzene-hexachloride

ABI Associate of the Institute of
Bookkeepers

ABIA Associate of the Bankers' Institute
of Australasia

ab init. *ab initio* (*L.* from the beginning)

ABIS Association of Burglary Insurance
Surveyors

abl. ablative

ABLA American Business Law
Association

ABLC Association of British Launderers and Cleaners

ABLS **1.** Association of British Library Schools **2.** Bachelor of Arts in Library Science

ABM **1.** anti-ballistic missile **2.** Associate in Business Management **3.** Australian Board of Missions

ABMEWS anti-ballistic missile early warning system

ABMEX Association of British Mining Equipment Exporters

ABMPM Association of British Manufacturers of Printers' Machinery

ABOCF Association of British Organic and Compound Fertilisers

ABP **1.** arterial blood pressure **2.** Associated Book Publishers

Abp. Archbishop

ABPA Australian Book Publishers' Association

ABPC American Book Publishers' Council

ABPI Association of the British Pharmaceutical Industry

ABPN Association of British Paediatric Nurses

ABPsS Associate of the British Psychological Society

abr. **1.** abridged **2.** abridgment

ABRO   Animal Breeding Research Organization, Edinburgh

ABRS   Association of British Riding Schools

ABRSM   Associated Board of the Royal Schools of Music

ABS   **1.** American Bible Society. **2.** American Bureau of Shipping **3.** Associate of the Building Societies Institute **4.** Association of Broadcasting Staff

abs.   **1.** absence **2.** absent **3.** absolute **4.** abstract

ABSM   Associate of the Birmingham School of Music

absol.   absolute

abs. re.   *absente reo* (*L.* the defendant being absent)

abstr.   abstract

ABSW   Association of British Science Writers

ABT   Association of Building Technicians

abt.   about

ABTA   **1.** Allied Brewery Traders' Association **2.** (ab'tə) Association of British Travel Agents **3.** Australian British Trade Association

ABTAPL   Association of British Theological and Philosophical Libraries

ABTSA Association of British Tree Surgeons and Arborists

ABTT Association of British Theatre Technicians

ABU Asian Broadcasting Union

ABus Associate in Business (US)

abv. above

ABZ Association of British Zoologists

AC 1. Advisory Committee 2. Aero Club 3. Air Command 4. Air Commodore 5. Air Control 6. Air Corps 7. Air Council 8. Aircraftman 9. Alpine Club 10. Alternating Current 11. Ambulance Corps 12. analog computer 13. analytical chemist 14. Annual Conference 15. *ante Christum* (L. before Christ) 16. Appeal Case 17. Appeal Court 18. Army Corps 19. Army Council 20. Artillery College 21. Arts Council 22. Assistant Commissioner 23. Athletic Club 24. Atlantic Charter 25. *Auditor Camerae* (L. Auditor of the Papal Treasury) 26. Companion of the Order of Australia

A/C 1. account 2. account current

Ac *Chem.* actinium

ac. 1. acre 2. activity

a.c. 1. *ante cibum* (L. before meals) 2. author's correction

ACA 1. Agricultural Cooperative

Association (now **ACMS**) **2.** Associate of
the Institute of Chartered Accountants (of
England and Wales) **3.** Australian Council
for Aeronautics

acad. **1.** academic **2.** academy

AC & AE Association of Chemical and
Allied Employers

ACAS **1.** (āʹkas) Advisory, Conciliation
and Arbitration Service **2.** Assistant Chief
of Air Staff

ACATS Association of Civil Aviation
Technical Staffs

ACC **1.** Administrative Coordination
Committee **2.** Advanced Communications
Course **3.** Air Coordinating Committee
(US) **4.** Army Catering Corps
5. Associated Chemical Companies

acc. **1.** acceleration **2.** accent
3. accepted **4.** accompanied
5. according **6.** account **7.** accusative

ACCA Association of Certified and
Corporate Accountants

Accad. Accademia

acce. acceptance

accel. *Mus. accelerando* (*It.* more
quickly)

ACCI Association of Chambers of
Commerce of Ireland

ACCO **1.** Associate of the Canadian

College of Organists **2.** Association of Child Care Officers

ACCOR Associated Chambers of Commerce of Rhodesia

ACCP American College of Chest Physicians

Accred. Accredited

ACCS Associate of the Corporation of Certified Secretaries

acct. account

accy. accountancy

ACE **1.** Allied Command Europe **2.** American Council on Education **3.** Association of Consulting Engineers **4.** Association of Cultural Exchange **5.** Australian College of Education

ACER Australian Council for Educational Research

ACF **1.** Agricultural Cooperative Federation **2.** Army Cadet Force **3.** *Automobile Club de France*

ACFA Army Cadet Force Association

ACG **1.** Assistant Chaplain-General **2.** automatic control gear

ACGB Arts Council of Great Britain

ACGFC Associate of the City and Guilds Finsbury College, London

ACGI Associate of the City and Guilds of London Institute

AChS   Associate of the Society of Chiropodists

ACI   **1.** Alloy Castings Institute **2.** Army Council Instruction **3.** Associate of the Clothing Institute **4.** Associate of the Institute of Commerce **5.** Association of Chambers of Commerce of Ireland **6.** *Automobile Club d'Italia*

ACIA   Associate of the Corporation of Insurance Agents

ACIAA   Australian Commercial and Industrial Artists' Association

ACIB   Associate of the Corporation of Insurance Brokers

ACIC   Aeronautical Charting and Information Center (US)

ACIGS   Assistant Chief of the Imperial General Staff

ACII   Associate of the Chartered Insurance Institute

ACIS   Associate of the Chartered Institute of Secretaries

ACIV   Associate of the Commonwealth Institute of Valuers

ACJP   Airways Corporations Joint Pensions

ack.   acknowledge(d)

ackt.   acknowledgment

ACLANT (ak'lənt)   Allied Command Atlantic

ACLP   Association of Contact Lens Practitioners

ACLS   **1.** American Council of Learned Societies **2.** Automatic Carrier Landing System

ACLU   American Civil Liberties Union

ACM   **1.** Air Chief Marshal **2.** Arab Common Market

ACMA   Associate of the Institute of Cost and Management Accountants

ACMC   Association of Canadian Medical Colleges

ACMET (ak′met)   Advisory Council on Middle East Trade

ACMF   Australian Commonwealth Military Forces

ACML   Anti Common Market League

ACMM   Associate of the Conservatorium of Music, Melbourne

ACMS   Agricultural Cooperation and Marketing Services

ACN   *ante Christum natum* (*L.* before the birth of Christ)

ACNS   Assistant Chief of Naval Staff

ACO   **1.** Admiralty Compass Observatory **2.** Association of Children's Officers

AComm   Associate in Commerce

ACommA   Associate of the Society of Commercial Accountants

ACOP Association of Chief Officers of Police

ACORD (ə kôrd′) Advisory Council on Research and Development

ACORN (ā′kôrn′) *DP* automatic check-out and recording network

ACOS 1. American College of Osteopathic Surgeons 2. Assistant Chief of Staff

ACP 1. American College of Pharmacists 2. American College of Physicians 3. Associate of the College of Preceptors 4. Association of Clinical Pathologists 5. Association of Correctors of the Press

ACPA Associate of the Institution of Certified Public Accountants

acpt. acceptance

ACR Admiral Commanding Reserves

ACRA Associate of the Corporation of Registered Accountants (US)

A/CRE Acting Commander Royal Engineers

ACRR American Council on Race Relations

ACRS Advisory Committee on Reactor Safeguards (US)

ACS 1. Admiral Commanding Submarines 2. Admiralty Computing Service 3. American Cancer Society 4. American Chemical Society

5. American College of Surgeons
6. Association of Commonwealth Students
7. Australian Computer Society
8. *Automobil Club der Schweiz*

ACSEA   Allied Command South East Asia

ACSIL   Admiralty Centre for Scientific Information and Liaison (now **NSTIC**)

ACSIR   Advisory Council for Scientific and Industrial Research

ACSN   Association of Collegiate Schools of Nursing

ACSP   Advisory Council on Scientific Policy

ACSTI   Advisory Committee for Scientific and Technical Information

ACT   1. Australian Capital Territory
2. Australian College of Theology

Act.   1. Acting 2. Actuary

act.   active

actg.   acting

ACTH   adrenocorticotrophic hormone, an anti-rheumatic drug

ACTO   Advisory Council on the Treatment of Offenders

ACTS   Associate of the Society of Certificated Teachers of Shorthand

ACTT   Association of Cinematograph, Television and Allied Technicians

ACTU   Australian Council of Trade Unions

ACU **1.** American Congregational Union **2.** Association of Commonwealth Universities **3.** Auto-Cycle Union

ACV **1.** actual cash value **2.** air cushion vehicle (hovercraft) **3.** Associate of the College of Violinists

ACW **1.** Aircraftwoman **2.** alternating continuous waves

ACWA Associate of the Institute of Cost and Works Accountants (now **ACMA**)

AD **1.** *Mil.* active duty **2.** air defence **3.** *anno Domini* (*L.* in the year of our Lord)

ad. **1.** adverb **2.** advertisement

ADA **1.** Agricultural Development Association **2.** Aluminium Development Association **3.** American Dental Association **4.** Americans for Democratic Action **5.** Atomic Development Authority **6.** Australian Dental Association

ADC **1.** advise duration and charge **2.** Aide-de-Camp **3.** Aid to Dependent Children **4.** Air Defense Command (US) **5.** Amateur Dramatic Club **6.** *DP* analog-to-digital converter **7.** Army Dental Corps (now **RADC**) **8.** automatic digital calculator

ADCC Air Defense Control Center (US)

add. **1.** addendum **2.** addition(al) **3.** address

ADDC Air Defense Direction Center (US)

ADES   Association of Directors of Education in Scotland

ADF   automatic direction finder

ad fin.   *ad finem* (*L.* near the end)

ADG   Assistant Director-General

ADGB   Air Defence of Great Britain

ADH   1. Assistant Director of Hygiene 2. Association of Dental Hospitals

ad inf.   *ad infinitum* (*L.* to infinity)

ad init.   *ad initium* (*L.* at the beginning)

ad int.   *ad interim* (*L.* in the meantime)

adj.   1. adjacent 2. adjective 3. adjoining 4. adjourned 5. adjudged 6. adjunct 7. adjustment 8. adjutant

Adjt.   Adjutant

Adjt.-Gen.   Adjutant-General

ADL   Assistant Director of Labour

ad lib.   *ad libitum* (*L.* at will)

ad loc.   *ad locum* (*L.* at the place)

ADLP   Australian Democratic Labour Party

Adm.   Admiral(ty)

adm.   1. administration 2. administrative 3. admitted

admin.   administration

ADMS   Assistant Director of Medical Services

admx.   administratrix

ADN   *IVR* People's Democratic Republic of Yemen

ADNA Assistant Director of Naval Accounts
ADNC Assistant Director of Naval Construction
ADNI Assistant Director of Naval Intelligence
ADO Association of Dispensing Opticians
ADOS Assistant Director of Ordnance Service
ADP 1. adenosine diphosphate 2. automatic data processing
ADPR Assistant Director of Public Relations
ADRA Animal Diseases Research Association
ADT Assistant Director of Transport
adv. 1. *ad valorem* (*L.* according to the value) 2. advance 3. advent 4. adverb 5. adverbial 6. *adversus* (*L.* against) 7. advertisement 8. advisory 9. advocate
ad val. *ad valorem* (*L.* according to the value)
ADVS Assistant Director of Veterinary Services
advt. advertisement
ADW 1. Air Defence Warning 2. Assistant Director of Works
AE 1. Aeronautical Engineer 2. Agricultural Engineer 3. Atomic Energy
ae. *aetatis* (*L.* at the age of)

AEA **1.** Actor's Equity Association (US)
2. Agricultural Education Association
3. Agricultural Engineers' Association
4. American Economic Association
5. Atomic Energy Authority
AEAF Allied Expeditionary Air Force
AE & P Ambassador Extraordinary and
Plenipotentiary
AEB Associated Examining Board
AEC **1.** Agricultural Executive
Committee **2.** Association of Education
Committees **3.** Atomic Energy
Commission (US)
AEd Associate in Education
AEE Atomic Energy Establishment
AEF **1.** Allied Expeditionary Force
2. Amalgamated Union of Engineering and
Foundry Workers **3.** American
Expeditionary Force **4.** Australian
Expeditionary Force
AEI **1.** American Express International
2. Associated Electrical Industries
AELTC All England Lawn Tennis Club
AENA All-England Netball Association
AEng Associate in Engineering
aer. **1.** aeronautics **2.** aeroplane
AERA American Educational Research
Association
AERE Atomic Energy Research
Establishment

AERI Agricultural Economics Research Institute

aeron. 1. aeronautical 2. aeronautics

AES Agricultural Economics Society

AET Associate in Electrical Technology

aet. *aetatis* (*L.* at the age of)

AEU Amalgamated Engineering Union (now **AUEW**)

AEW 1. Admiralty Experimental Works 2. airborne early warning

AF 1. Admiral of the Fleet 2. Air Force 3. Anglo-French 4. Associated Fisheries 5. Associate Fellow 6. audio-frequency

A/F as found (in auction catalogues)

AFA 1. Air Force Association (US) 2. Amateur Fencing Association 3. Amateur Football Association 4. Associate in Fine Arts 5. Associate of the Faculty of Actuaries (Scotland) 6. Associate of the Faculty of Auditors

AFAIM Associate Fellow of the Australian Institute of Management

AF & AM Ancient Free and Accepted Masons

AFAS Associate of the Faculty of Architects and Surveyors

AFB 1. Air Force Base 2. American Foundation for the Blind

AFBS American and Foreign Bible Society

AFC 1. Air Force Cross 2. Association

Football Club **3.** Australian Flying Corps
(now **RAAF**) **4.** automatic frequency
control

AFCAI   Associate Fellow of the Canadian
Aeronautical Institute

AFCE   Associate in Fuel Technology and
Chemical Engineering

AFCENT (af'sent)   Allied Forces Central
Europe

AFCR   American Federation for Clinical
Research

AFCU   American and Foreign Christian
Union

AFD   **1.** accelerated freeze drying
2. Doctor of Fine Arts

AFEE   Airborne Forces Experimental
Establishment

AFEX   Armed Forces Exchange (US)

affil.   affiliated

afft.   affidavit

AFG   *IVR* Afghanistan

Afg.   Afghanistan

AFHQ   Allied Forces Headquarters

AFI   **1.** American Film Institute
2. Associate of the Faculty of Insurance

AFIA   **1.** American Foreign Insurance
Association **2.** Associate of the Federal
Institute of Accountants (Aust.)

AFIAS   Associate Fellow of the Institute of
the Aerospace Sciences (US)

AFII American Federation of International Institutes
AFIIM Associate Fellow of the Institute of Industrial Managers
AFL-CIO American Federation of Labor and Congress of Industrial Organizations
AFM **1.** Air Force Medal **2.** American Federation of Musicians
AFMED (af'med) Allied Forces Mediterannean
AFN **1.** American Forces Network **2.** Armed Forces Network
AFNE Allied Forces Northern Europe
Afr. Africa(n)
AFRAeS Associate Fellow of the Royal Aeronautical Society
Afrik. Afrikaans
AFRTS Armed Forces Radio and Television Service (US)
AFS **1.** American Field Service **2.** Associate Surveyor Member of the Faculty of Architects and Surveyors **3.** Auxiliary Fire Service
afsd. aforesaid
AFT American Federation of Teachers
AFTE American Federation of Technical Engineers
AFTM American Foundation of Tropical Medicine

AFTRA   American Federation of Television and Radio Artists

AFULE   Australian Federated Union of Locomotive Enginemen

AFV   armoured fighting vehicle

AG   **1.** Adjutant General **2.** Attorney General

Ag   *Chem.* silver

AGA   Amateur Gymnastics Association

AGARD   Advisory Group for Aeronautical Research and Development

AGC   automatic gain control

AGCA   automatic ground controlled approach

AGCL   automatic ground controlled landing

agcy.   agency

AGE   Associate in General Education

AGF   Adjutant-General to the Forces

AGM   **1.** air-to-ground missile **2.** Annual General Meeting

AGMA   American Guild of Musical Artists

AGR   advanced gas-cooled reactor

agr., agric.   **1.** agricultural **2.** agriculture

AGS   **1.** American Geographical Society **2.** American Gynaecological Society

AGSM   Associate of the Guildhall School of Music and Drama

AGSRO   Association of Government Supervisors and Radio Officers

agst. against
agt. 1. agent 2. agreement
AGU American Geophysical Union
AGVA American Guild of Variety Artists
a.g.w. actual gross weight
AH *anno Hegirae* (*L.* in the year of the Hegira)
a.h. ampere hour
AHA 1. American Heart Association
2. American Historical Association
3. American Hospital Association
4. American Hotel Association
5. American Humane Association
6. Associate of the Institute of Hospital Administrators 7. Australian Hotels Association
AHE Association for Higher Education (US)
AHI 1. American Health Institute
2. American Hospital Institute
a.h.l. *ad hunc locum* (*L.* at this place)
AHMC Association of Hospital Management Committees
AHQ 1. Air Headquarters 2. Army Headquarters
a.h.v. *ad hunc vocem* (*L.* at this word)
AHWA Association of Hospital and Welfare Administrators
AHWC Associate of the Heriot-Watt College

AI **1.** Amnesty International **2.** artificial insemination

a.i. *ad interim* (*L*. in the meantime)

AIA **1.** Aerospace Industries Association of America **2.** American Institute of Architects **3.** Archaeological Institute of America **4.** Associate of the Institute of Actuaries **5.** Association of International Accountants **6.** Aviation Industry Association (NZ)

AIAA **1.** American Institute of Aeronautics and Astronautics **2.** Associate Architect Member of the Incorporated Association of Architects and Surveyors **3.** Associate of the Institute of Accountants and Actuaries **4.** Association of International Advertising Agencies

AIAE Associate of the Institution of Automobile Engineers

AIAgrE Associate of the Institution of Agricultural Engineers

AIAL Associate Member of the International Institute of Arts and Letters

AIANZ Associate of the Incorporated Institute of Accountants, New Zealand

AIArb Associate of the Institute of Arbitrators

AIAS **1.** Associate Surveyor Member of the Incorporated Association of Architects

and Surveyors **2.** Australian Institute of
Agricultural Science

AIB **1.** American Institute of Banking
2. Associate of the Institute of Bankers
3. Associate of the Institute of Building
4. Association of Insurance Brokers

AIBA American Industrial Bankers'
Association

AIBP Associate of the Institute of British
Photographers

AIBS American Institute of Biological
Sciences

AIC **1.** Agricultural Institute of Canada
2. American Institute of Chemists
3. Association of Independent Cinemas

AICA **1.** Associate Member of the
Commonwealth Institute of Accountants
2. Associate of the Institute of Company
Accountants

AICC All-India Congress Committee

AICE **1.** American Institute of Chemical
Engineers **2.** American Institute of
Consulting Engineers **3.** Associate of the
Institution of Civil Engineers

AICPA American Institute of Certified
Public Accountants

AICS Associate of the Institute of
Chartered Shipbrokers

AID **1.** acute infectious disease **2.** (ād)
Agency for International Development

(US) **3.** American Institute of Decorators
4. Army Intelligence Department
5. artificial insemination by donor
AIDC   American Industrial Development Council
AIDIA   Associate of the Industrial Design Institute of America
AIEE   Associate of the Institution of Electrical Engineers
AIER   American Institute of Economic Research
AIF   Australian Imperial Force
AIFA   Associate of the International Faculty of Arts
AIFM   Associate of the Institute of Factory Managers
AIFS   American Institute for Foreign Study
AIFT   American Institute for Foreign Trade
AIGA   American Institute of Graphic Arts
AIGM   Associate of the Institute of General Managers
AIH   artificial insemination by husband
AIHA   Associate of the Institute of Hospital Administrators
AIHsg   Associate of the Institute of Housing
AIHVE   Associate of the Institution of Heating and Ventilating Engineers

AIIA 1. Associate of the Institute of Industrial Administration 2. Associate of the Insurance Institute of America 3. Australian Institute of International Affairs

AIIAL Associate of the International Institute of Arts and Letters

AIIE American Institute of Industrial Engineers

AIITech Associate Member of the Institute of Industrial Technicians

AIL Associate of the Institute of Linguists

AILA 1. Associate of the Institute of Land Agents 2. Associate of the Institute of Landscape Architects

AILocoE Associate of the Institution of Locomotive Engineers

AIM 1. African Inland Mission 2. American Institute of Management 3. Associate of the Institution of Metallurgists 4. Australian Inland Mission 5. Australian Institute of Management

AIMarE Associate of the Institute of Marine Engineers

AIME 1. American Institute of Mining and Metallurgical Engineers 2. Associate of the Institution of Mining Engineers

AIMechE Associate of the Institution of Mechanical Engineers

AIMI Associate of the Institute of the Motor Industry

AIMinE Associate of the Institution of Mining Engineers

AIMM 1. Associate of the Institution of Mining and Metallurgy 2. Australasian Institute of Mining and Metallurgy

AIMO Association of Industrial Medical Officers

AIMPE Australian Institute of Marine and Power Engineers

AIMTA Associate of the Institute of Municipal Treasurers and Accountants

AInstCE Associate of the Institution of Civil Engineers

AInstP Associate of the Institute of Physics

AIOB Associate of the Institute of Building

AIP American Institute of Physics

AIPE 1. American Institute of Plant Engineers 2. Associate of the Institution of Production Engineers

AIPet Associate of the Institute of Petroleum

AIPHE Associate of the Institution of Public Health Engineers

AIQ Associate of the Institute of Quarrying

AIQS Associate of the Institute of Quantity Surveyors

AIR 1. All-India Radio 2. American Institute for Research

AIRTE Associate of the Institute of Road Transport Engineers

AIS 1. Associate of the Institute of Statisticians 2. Australasian Institute of Secretaries 3. Australian Iron and Steel

AISA Associate of the Incorporated Secretaries' Association

AISI 1. American Iron and Steel Institute 2. Associate of the Iron and Steel Institute

AIST Associate of the Institute of Science and Technology

AIStructE Associate of the Institution of Structural Engineers

AIT 1. Association of HM Inspectors of Taxes 2. Association of Investment Trusts

AIWE Associate of the Institution of Water Engineers

AIWM American Institute of Weights and Measures

AJA Australian Journalists' Association

AJC Australian Jockey Club

a.k.a. also known as

AKC 1. American Kennel Club 2. Associate of King's College, London

AL 1. *IVR* Albania 2. American League 3. American Legion 4. Anglo-Latin

Al *Chem.* aluminium
al. alcohol(ic)
ALA 1. American Library Association
2. Associate in Liberal Arts 3. Associate
of the Library Association 4. Authors'
League of America 5. Automobile Legal
Association
Ala. Alabama
ALAA 1. Associate of the Library
Association of Australia 2. Associate of
the London Association of Certified
Accountants
ALAM Associate of the London Academy
of Music
ALAS Associate of the Land Agents'
Society
Alas. Alaska
Alb. Albania(n)
Alba. Alberta
Alban. *Albaniensis* (*L.* of St Albans)
ALBM air-launched ballistic missile
ALCAN (al'kan) Aluminium Company of
Canada
ALCD Associate of the London College of
Divinity
ALCM Associate of the London College of
Music
Ald. Alderman
ALG antilymphocyte globulin
Alg. Algeria(n)

alg. algebra
ALGES Association of Local Government Engineers and Surveyors
ALGFO Association of Local Government Financial Officers
ALGOL (al'gol) *DP algorithmic language*
ALI American Library Institute
alk. alkali
ALM *Artium Liberalium Magister* (*L.* Master of the Liberal Arts)
ALO Asian Labour Organization
ALP 1. American Labor Party
2. Australian Labour Party
ALPA Air Line Pilots' Association (US)
ALPO Association of Land and Property Owners
ALRA Abortion Law Reform Association
ALS Associate of the Linnean Society
alt. 1. alteration 2. alternate
3. alternative 4. altitude 5. alto
Alta. Alberta
alter. alteration
ALTU Association of Liberal Trade Unionists
alum. aluminium
AM 1. Air Marshal 2. Air Ministry
3. Albert Medal 4. amplitude modulation
5. *anno mundi* (*L.* in the year of the world)
6. *ante meridiem* (*L.* before noon)
7. arithmetic mean 8. *Artium Magister* (*L.*

Master of Arts) **9.** Associate Member
10. *Ave Maria* **11.** Member of the Order
of Australia

Am   *Chem.* americium

Am.   America(n)

a.m.   *ante meridiem*

AMA   **1.** American Management
Association **2.** American Medical
Association **3.** Assistant Masters'
Association **4.** Australian Medical
Association

AMAB   Army Medical Advisory Board

AMAIMM   Associate Member of the
Australasian Institute of Mining and
Metallurgy

amal.   amalgamated

AMAmIEE   Associate Member of the
American Institute of Electrical Engineers

Amb.   Ambassador

AMBAC   Associate Member of the British
Association of Chemists

AMBIM   Associate Member of the British
Institute of Management

AMC   **1.** American Motors Corporation
2. Army Medical Corps (now **RAMC**)

AMCIA   Associate Member of the
Association of Cost and Industrial
Accountants

AMCIB   Associate Member of the
Corporation of Insurance Brokers

AMDG *ad majorem Dei gloriam* (*L.* to the greater glory of God)
AME **1.** Advanced Master of Education **2.** African Methodist Episcopal
AMEIC Associate Member of the Engineering Institute of Canada
Amer. America(n)
AMES Air Ministry Experimental Station
AMet Associate of Metallurgy
AMF **1.** Australian Marine Force **2.** Australian Military Forces
AMG Allied Military Government
AMHCI Associate Member of the Hotel and Catering Institute
AMIA Associate Member of the Institute of Almoners
AMIAE Associate Member of the Institute of Aeronautical Engineers
AMICE Associate Member of the Institution of Civil Engineers
AMICEI Associate Member of the Institution of Civil Engineers of Ireland
AMIChemE Associate Member of the Institution of Chemical Engineers
AMIEA Associate Member of the Institution of Engineers, Australia
AMIEE Associate Member of the Institution of Electrical Engineers
AMIERE Associate Member of the

Institution of Electronic and Radio
Engineers

AMIFireE   Associate Member of the
Institution of Fire Engineers

AMIGasE   Associate Member of the
Institute of Gas Engineers

AMIH   Associate Member of the Institute
of Housing

AMIHVE   Associate Member of the
Institute of Heating and Ventilating
Engineers

AMIIA   Associate Member of the Institute
of Industrial Administration

AMILocoE   Associate Member of the
Institution of Locomotive Engineers

AMIMarE   Associate Member of the
Institute of Marine Engineers

AMIME   Associate Member of the
Institution of Mining Engineers

AMIMechE   Associate Member of the
Institution of Mechanical Engineers

AMIMI   Associate Member of the Institute
of the Motor Industry

AMIMinE   Associate Member of the
Institution of Mining Engineers

AMIMM   Associate Member of the
Institution of Mining and Metallurgy

AMIMunE   Associate Member of the
Institution of Municipal Engineers

AMInstBE Associate Member of the
Institution of British Engineers

AMInstEE American Institute of
Electrical Engineers

AMInstHE Associate Member of the
Institution of Highway Engineers

AMInstPC Associate Member of the
Institute of Public Cleansing

AMInstR Associate Member of the
Institute of Refrigeration

AMInstT Associate Member of the
Institute of Transport

AMInstTE Associate Member of the
Institution of Transport Engineers

AMINucE Associate Member of the
Institution of Nuclear Engineers

AMIOB Associate Member of the
Institute of Building

AMIOP Associate Member of the Institute
of Printing

AMIPHE Associate Member of the
Institution of Public Health Engineers

AMIPlantE Associate Member of the
Institution of Plant Engineers

AMIPM Associate Member of the
Institute of Personnel Management

AMIProdE Associate Member of the
Institute of Production Engineers

AMIPtgM Associate Member of the
Institute of Printing Management

AMIStructE   Associate Member of the
Institution of Structural Engineers
AMITA   Associate Member of the
Industrial Transport Association
AMIWE   Associate Member of the
Institute of Water Engineers
AMIWM   Associate Member of the
Institute of Works Managers
AMLS   Master of Arts in Library Science
AMM   anti-missile missile
AMMI   American Merchant Marine
Institute
Amn.   Airman
amn.   amunition
AMNZIE   Associate Member of the New
Zealand Institution of Engineers
AMP   **1.** adenosine monophosphate
2. Australian Mutual Provident Society
amp.   **1.** amperage **2.** ampere
3. amplifier **4.** amplitude
AMPA   Associate of the Master
Photographers' Association of Great Britain
AMPAS   Academy of Motion Picture Arts
and Sciences (US)
AMRINA   Associate Member of the Royal
Institution of Naval Architects
AMRTS   Associate Member of the Royal
Television Society
AMRW   Air Ministry Radio Station
AMS   **1.** Ancient Monuments Society

2. Army Medical Staff **3.** Association of Medical Secretaries **4.** Australian Medical Services

AMSE Associate Member of the Society of Engineers

AMSO Association of Market Survey Organizations

AMSW Master of Arts in Social Work

AMT **1.** Academy of Medicine, Toronto **2.** Air Mail Transfer **3.** Associate in Mechanical Technology **4.** Associate in Medical Technology **5.** Association of Marine Traders **6.** Master of Arts in Teaching

amt. amount

AMTPI Associate Member of the Town Planning Institute

AMU atomic mass unit

AMus Associate in Music

AMusD Doctor of Musical Arts

AMWA American Medical Writers' Association

AN **1.** Anglo-Norman **2.** Associate in Nursing

An *Chem.* actinon

an. **1.** *anno* (*L.* in the year) **2.** anonymous **3.** *ante* (*L.* before)

ANA **1.** Australian National Airways **2.** Australian Natives' Association

anag. anagram

anal.   **1.** analogous   **2.** analogy
   3. analysis   **4.** analytic

ANARE   Australian National Antarctic Research Expedition

anat.   **1.** anatomical   **2.** anatomist
   3. anatomy

ANC   **1.** African National Congress
   2. Army Nursing Corps   **3.** Australian Newspaper Council

anc.   ancient(ly)

ANCUN   Australian National Committee for the United Nations

AND   *IVR* Andorra

and.   *Mus.* (*It. andante*) moderately slow

ANF   Atlantic Nuclear Force

Angl.   **1.** Anglican   **2.** Anglicized

anim.   *Mus.* (*It. animato*) animated

ann.   **1.** annual   **2.** annuity

anniv.   anniversary

annot.   **1.** annotated   **2.** annotation
   3. annotator

anon.   anonymous

ANP   Australian Nationalist Party

ANPA   American Newspaper Publishers' Association

ANRC   **1.** American National Red Cross
   2. Australian National Research Council

ANS   **1.** American Nuclear Society
   2. Army Nursing Service

ans.   answer

ANSI American National Standards Institute

ANSL Australian National Standards Laboratory

ANSP Australian National Socialist Party

ant. 1. antenna 2. antiquarian 3. antique 4. antonym

ANTA 1. American National Theatre and Academy 2. Australian National Travel Association

anthol. anthology

anthrop. 1. anthropological 2. anthropology

antiq. 1. antiquarian 2. antiquity

ANU Australian National University

ANZAAS Australian and New Zealand Association for the Advancement of Science

ANZAC (an'zak') Australian and New Zealand Army Corps

ANZIA Associate of the New Zealand Institute of Architects

ANZIC Associate of the New Zealand Institute of Chemists

ANZLA Associate of the New Zealand Library Association

AO 1. Army Order 2. Officer of the Order of Australia

a/o account of

AOA Association of Official Architects

AOB any other business

AOC   Air Officer Commanding
AOCB   any other competent business
AOC-in-C   Air Officer Commanding-in-Chief
AOD   1. Ancient Order of Druids 2. Army Ordnance Department
AOF   1. Ancient Order of Foresters 2. Australian Olympic Federation
AOH   Ancient Order of Hibernians
AOP   Association of Optical Practitioners
aor.   aorist
AOS   Ancient Order of Shepherds
AOSW   Association of Official Shorthand Writers
AOT   American Ornithologists' Union
AP   1. Air Police 2. American Pharmacopoeia 3. Andhra Pradesh 4. *ante prandium* (*L.* before meals) 5. armour-piercing 6. Associated Press 7. atmospheric pressure 8. author's proof
Ap.   1. Apostle 2. April
ap.   apothecary
a.p.   1. above proof 2. author's proof
APA   1. All Parties Administration (Aust.) 2. American Pharmaceutical Association 3. American Philological Association 4. American Physicists' Association 5. American Press Association 6. American Protective Association 7. American Protestant

APAC

Association **8.** American Psychiatric Association **9.** American Psychological Association **10.** Associate in Public Administration **11.** Association for the Prevention of Addiction **12.** Australian Physiotherapy Association
APAC Association of Patternmakers and Allied Craftsmen
APAE Association of Public Address Engineers
APANZ Associate of the Public Accountants of New Zealand
APB all points bulletin
APBF Accredited Poultry Breeders' Federation
APC **1.** automatic phase control **2.** automatic pitch control
APD **1.** Army Pay Department **2.** *Authors' and Printers' Dictionary*
APDE Association of Painting and Decorating Employers
APEX **1.** (ā'peks) Advance Purchase Excursion **2.** Association of Professional, Executive, Clerical and Computer Staff
aph. aphorism
APHI Association of Public Health Inspectors
API American Petroleum Institute
APLE Association of Public Lighting Engineers

APM 1. Assistant Paymaster
2. Assistant Provost Marshal
APMC Allied Political and Military
Commission
APMG Assistant Postmaster General
APO 1. Acting Pilot Officer 2. Army
Post Office
apo. apogee
Apoc. 1. Apocalypse 2. *Bib.* Apocrypha
apos. apostrophe
app. 1. apparatus 2. apparent
3. appendix 4. applied 5. appointed
6. apprentice 7. approved
8. approximate
appro. 1. approbation 2. approval
approx. approximate(ly)
apptd. appointed
APPU Australian Primary Producers'
Union
Apr. April
APRA Australian Performing Right
Association
APRC *anno post Romam conditam* (*L.* in
the year after the founding of Rome, 753
BC)
APRL Association for the Preservation of
Rural Life
APRS Association for the Preservation of
Rural Scotland
APS 1. American Peace Society

2. American Philatelic Society
3. American Philosophical Society
4. American Physical Society **5.** American Protestant Society **6.** Associate of the Pharmaceutical Society
APSA **1.** American Political Science Association **2.** Australian Political Studies Association
APSW Association of Psychiatric Social Workers
APT **1.** advanced passenger train
2. Association of Printing Technologists
3. Association of Private Traders
apt. apartment
APTU African Postal and Telecommunications Union
APU Arab Postal Union
APWU Amalgamated Postal Workers' Union
AQ achievement quotient
aq. *aqua* (*L.* water)
AQC Associate of Queen's College, London
AQMG Assistant Quartermaster General
AR **1.** Airman Recruit (US) **2.** Army Regulation **3.** Autonomous Republic
Ar *Chem.* argon
Ar. **1.** Arabic **2.** Aramaic
ar. **1.** arrival **2.** arrives
a.r. *anno regni* (*L.* in the year of the reign)

ARA **1.** Agricultural Research Administration **2.** Aircraft Research Association **3.** American Railway Association **4.** Associate of the Royal Academy

Arab **1.** Arabian **2.** Arabic

ARAC Associate of the Royal Agricultural College

ARACI Associate of the Royal Australian Chemical Institute

ARAD Associate of the Royal Academy of Dancing

ARAeS Associate of the Royal Aeronautical Society

ARAIA Associate of the Royal Australian Institute of Architects

ARAM Associate of the Royal Academy of Music

Aram. Aramaic

ARAMCO (ə ram′kō) Arabian-American Oil Company

ARAS Associate of the Royal Astronomical Society

ARB **1.** Air Registration Board **2.** Air Research Bureau

arb. **1.** arbiter **2.** arbitration

ARBA Associate of the Royal Society of British Artists

ARBS Associate of the Royal Society of British Sculptors

ARC **1.** Aeronautical Research Council
2. Agricultural Research Council
3. American Red Cross **4.** automatic relay
calculator **5.** Automobile Racing Club

ARCA Associate of the Royal College of
Art

arc cos *Math.* inverse cosine

Arch. **1.** Archbishop **2.** Archdeacon
3. Archduke **4.** Archipelago
5. Architecture

arch. **1.** archaic **2.** archaism
3. archery **4.** archipelago **5.** architect
6. architecture **7.** archive

archaeol. archaeology

Archd. **1.** Archdeacon **2.** Archduke

ArchE Architectural Engineer

archit. architecture

ARCM Associate of the Royal College of
Music

ARCO Associate of the Royal College of
Organists

ARCOS Anglo-Russian Cooperative
Society

ARCS **1.** Associate of the Royal College
of Science **2.** Associate of the Royal
College of Surgeons **3.** Australian Red
Cross Society

arc sin *Math.* inverse sine

ARCST Associate of the Royal College of

Science and Technology of Glasgow (now University of Strathclyde)

arc tan   *Math.* inverse tangent

ARCVS   Associate of the Royal College of Veterinary Surgeons

ARD   acute respiratory disease

ARDC   Air Research and Development Command (US)

ARDE   Armament Research and Development Establishment

ARDI   Association of Registered Driving Instructors

ARE   Associate in Religious Education

ARELS (ar'əlz)   Association of Recognised English Language Schools

Arg.   **1.** Argentina **2.** Argyllshire (former county)

arg.   *argentum* (*L.* silver)

ARIBA   Associate of the Royal Institute of British Architects

ARIC   Associate of the Royal Institute of Chemistry

ARICS   Associate of the Royal Institution of Chartered Surveyors

ARINA   Associate of the Royal Institution of Naval Architects

ARIPHH   Associate of the Royal Institute of Public Health and Hygiene

arith.   arithmetic(al)

Ariz.   Arizona

Ark. Arkansas
ARL 1. Admiralty Research Laboratory
2. Aeronautical Research Laboratory
ARM anti-radar missile
ArM Master of Architecture
Arm. 1. Armenia(n) 2. Armoric
ARMIT Associate of the Royal Melbourne Institute of Technology
ARNO Association of Retired Naval Officers
ARP 1. air raid precautions
2. Australian Republican Party
ARPS Associate of the Royal Photographic Society
ARR 1. *anno regni regis* or *reginae* (*L.* in the year of the king's *or* queen's reign)
2. Association for Radiation Research
arr. 1. arranged 2. arrangement
3. arrival
ARRC Associate of the Royal Red Cross
ARRL American Radio Relay League
ARSA 1. Associate of the Royal Scottish Academy 2. Associate of the Royal Society of Arts
ARSL Associate of the Royal Society of Literature
ARSM Associate of the Royal School of Mines
art. 1. article 2. artificial 3. artillery
ARTC Air Route Traffic Control

arty. artillery

ARU **1.** American Railway Union **2.** Australian Railways Union

ARV American Revised Version (of the Bible)

ARVIA Associate of the Royal Victorian Institute of Architects

ARWS Associate of the Royal Society of Painters in Water Colours

AS **1.** Anglo-Saxon **2.** *anno salutis* (*L.* in the year of salvation) **3.** anti-submarine **4.** Assistant Secretary **5.** Associate in Science

As *Chem.* arsenic

As. **1.** Asia(n) **2.** Asiatic

ASA **1.** Advertising Standards Authority **2.** Amateur Swimming Association **3.** American Standards Association (now **ANSI**) **4.** American Statistical Association **5.** Atomic Scientists' Association

ASAA Associate of the Society of Incorporated Accountants and Auditors (now incorporated with **ACA**)

a.s.a.p. as soon as possible

ASAT Anti-Satellite (Satellite)

ASB Air Safety Board (US)

ASBU Arab States Broadcasting Union

ASC **1.** American Society of

Cinematographers **2.** Army Service Corps
(now **RCT**)
ASc Associate in Science
ASCAP (as'kap) American Society of
Composers, Authors, and Publishers
ASCEA American Society of Civil
Engineers and Architects
ASCII *DP* American Standard Code for
Information Interchange
ASDIC (az'dik) Allied Submarine Detection
Investigation Committee
ASE **1.** Amalgamated Society of
Engineers **2.** American Stock Exchange
3. Army School of Education
4. Association for Science Education
a.s.e. air standard efficiency
ASEAN Association of South-East Asian
Nations
ASF Associate of the Institute of Shipping
and Fowarding Agents
ASGB Aeronautical Society of Great
Britain
ASH (ash) Action on Smoking and Health
ASI air speed indicator
ASL Acting Sub-Lieutenant
ASLEF (az'lef) Associated Society of
Locomotive Engineers and Firemen
ASLIB (az'lib) Association of Special
Libraries and Information Bureaus

ASLP   Amalgamated Society of Lithographic Printers

ASM   air-to-surface missile

ASME   American Society of Mechanical Engineers

ASN   Army Service Number

ASPAC   Asian and South Pacific Council

ASPCA   American Society for the Prevention of Cruelty to Animals

ASS   **1.** Associate in Secretarial Science **2.** Associate in Secretarial Studies

Ass.   Assembly

ass.   **1.** assistant **2.** association **3.** assorted

Asscn., Assn.   Association

ASSET (as'et)   Association of Supervisory Staffs Executives and Technicians

Assoc.   Associate

ASSR   Autonomous Soviet Socialist Republic

asst.   assistant

Assyr.   Assyrian

AST   Atlantic Standard Time

ASTA   American Society of Travel Agents

ASTM   **1.** American Society for Testing and Materials **2.** American Society of Tropical Medicine

ASTMS   Association of Scientific, Technical, and Managerial Staffs

astr. **1.** astronomer **2.** astronomical
3. astronomy
ASTRO (as'trō)   Air Space Travel
Research Organization (US)
astrol. **1.** astrologer **2.** astrological
3. astrology
astron. **1.** astronomer **2.** astronomical
3. astronomy
ASTUC   Anglo-Soviet Trades Union
Committee
ASU   American Students' Union
ASVA   Associate of the Incorporated
Society of Valuers and Auctioneers
ASW **1.** anti-submarine warfare
2. Association of Scientific Workers
ASWD & KW   Amalgamated Society of
Wire Drawers and Kindred Workers
AT **1.** alternative technology **2.** anti-tank
At *Chem.* astatine
at. **1.** airtight **2.** atmosphere **3.** atomic
ATA **1.** Air Transport Association **2.** Air
Transport Auxiliary **3.** American
Transport Association **4.** Atlantic Treaty
Association
ATC **1.** Air Traffic Control **2.** Air
Training Corps **3.** automatic train control
ATech   Associate in Technology
ATI **1.** Associate of the Textile Institute
2. Association of Technical Institutions
Atl.   Atlantic

atm.   **1.** atmosphere **2.** atmospheric

at. no.   atomic number

ATP   adenosine triphosphate

ATS   **1.** *DP* Administrative Terminal System **2.** American Temperance Society **3.** American Tract Society **4.** American Transport Service **5.** anti-tetanus serum **6.** Auxiliary Territorial Service (now **WRAC**)

a.t.s.   *Law* at the suit of

Att.   Attorney

att.   **1.** attached **2.** attention **3.** attorney

attn.   attention

attrib.   **1.** attribute **2.** attributive

atty.   attorney

Atty. Gen.   Attorney General

ATUC   African Trade Union Confederation

ATV   Associated Television

at. vol.   atomic volume

at. wt.   atomic weight

AU   **1.** Ångström unit **2.** astronomical unit

Au   *Chem.* gold

AUA   American Unitarian Association

AUAW   Amalgamated Union of Asphalt Workers

AUBTW   Amalgamated Union of Building Trade Workers

AUC   Australian Universities Commission

a.u.c. **1.** *ab urbe condita* (*L.* from the founding of the city of Rome, 753 BC) **2.** *anno urbis conditae* (*L.* in a specified year from the founding of the city)

aud. audit(or)

AUEW Amalgamated Union of Engineering Workers

Aug. August

aug. augmentative

AULLA Australasian Universities Language and Literature Association

AUM air-to-underwater missile

AUS **1.** Army of the United States **2.** *IVR* Australia

Aust. Australia(n)

Austl. Australasia

AUT Association of University Teachers

aut. automatic

auth. **1.** author **2.** authority **3.** authorized

Auth. Ver. Authorized Version (of the Bible)

auto. **1.** automatic **2.** automobile **3.** automotive

aux. auxiliary

AV **1.** arteriovenous **2.** arterioventricular **3.** Artillery Volunteers **4.** audio-visual **5.** auriculoventricular **6.** Authorized Version (of the Bible)

Av. Avenue
av. **1.** average **2.** avoirdupois
a.v. *ad valorem* (*L.* according to the value)
AVA Australian Veterinary Association
avdp. avoirdupois
Ave. Avenue
avg. average
AVM Air Vice-Marshal
avn. aviation
AVR Army Volunteer Reserve
AVS Anti-Vivisection Society
AW Articles of War
a.w. atomic weight
AWA Amalgamated Wireless (Australasia)
AWB Australian Wool Board
AWF American Wildlife Federation
AWOL (ā′wol′) absent without official leave
AWRE Atomic Weapons Research Establishment
AWU **1.** Agricultural Workers' Union (SAfr) **2.** Australian Workers' Union
ax. **1.** axiom **2.** axis
AYH American Youth Hostels
az. azimuth

B

B 1. Bachelor 2. bacillus 3. Baron
4. base 5. *Mus.* bass 6. Battery 7. bay
8. *IVR* Belgium 9. Bible 10. bicuspid
11. *Chess* bishop 12. Black 13. Blessed
14. bolivar 15. boliviano 16. Bomber
17. book 18. born 19. *Chem.* boron
20. *Cricket* bowled 21. breadth
22. British 23. Brother

BA 1. *Baccalaureus Artium* (*L.* Bachelor
of Arts) 2. Board of Agriculture
3. Booksellers' Association 4. British
Academy 5. British Airways 6. British
America 7. British Association 8. Buenos
Aires

Ba *Chem.* barium

BAA 1. Bachelor of Applied Arts
2. Bachelor of Art and Architecture
3. British Airports Authority 4. British
Archaeological Association 5. British
Astronomical Association

BAA & A British Association of
Accountants and Auditors

BAAB British Amateur Athletic Board

BAAS British Association for the
Advancement of Science

Bab. Babylon(ian)

BABA   beam *or* blind approach beacon system

BAC   **1.** British Aircraft Corporation **2.** British Association of Chemists

BACC   British American Chamber of Commerce (US)

BAcc   Bachelor of Accountancy

Bach.   Bachelor

BACIE   British Association for Commercial and Industrial Education

back.   backwardation

BACM   British Association of Colliery Management

BACO (bā′kō)   British Aluminium Company Ltd.

BACR   British Association for Cancer Research

bact.   **1.** bacteria **2.** bacteriology **3.** bacterium

bacteriol.   **1.** bacteriological **2.** bacteriology

BAD   British Association of Dermatology

BADA   British Antique Dealers' Association

BAdmEng   Bachelor of Administrative Engineering

BAdmin   Bachelor of Administration

BAE   **1.** Bachelor of Aeronautical Engineering **2.** Bachelor of Agricultural Engineering **3.** Bachelor of Architectural

Engineering **4.** Bachelor of Arts in Education **5.** Bureau of Agricultural Economics (US).

BAEA   British Actors' Equity Association

BAeE   Bachelor of Aeronautical Engineering

BAFM   British Association of Forensic Medicine

BAFO   British Army Forces Overseas

BAGA   British Amateur Gymnastics Association

BAgE   Bachelor of Agricultural Engineering

BAgr   Bachelor of Agriculture

BAgSc   Bachelor of Agricultural Science

Bah.   Bahamas

BAI   *Baccalaureus in Arte Ingeniaria* (*L.* Bachelor of Engineering)

BAJour   Bachelor of Arts in Journalism

BAL   **1.** *DP* basic assembly language **2.** *Chem.* British Anti-Lewisite

bal.   balance

ball.   **1.** ballast **2.** ballistics

BALPA (bal'pə)   British Air Line Pilots' Association

Balt.   **1.** Baltic **2.** Baltimore

BAM   **1.** Bachelor of Applied Mathematics **2.** Bachelor of Arts in Music

BAN   British Association of Neurologists

B & B   bed and breakfast

B & FBS   British and Foreign Bible Society
b & s   brandy and soda
b & w   black and white
BAO   **1.** *Baccalaureus Artis Obstetricae*
(*L.* Bachelor of Obstetrics) **2.** Bachelor of
Arts in Oratory
BAOR   British Army of the Rhine
Bap.   Baptist
bap.   baptized
BAPS   **1.** British Association of Paediatric
Surgeons **2.** British Association of Plastic
Surgeons
BAR   Browning automatic rifle
Bar.   *Bib.* Baruch
bar.   **1.** barometer **2.** barometric
3. barrel **4.** barrister
BArch   Bachelor of Architecture
barit.   baritone
barr.   barrister
Bart.   Baronet
BAS   **1.** Bachelor in Agricultural Science
2. Bachelor of Applied Science **3.** British
Acoustical Society **4.** British Antarctic
Survey **5.** Building Advisory Service
BASc   **1.** Bachelor of Agricultural
Science **2.** Bachelor of Applied Science
BASIC (bā′sik)   *DP* Beginners' All-
purpose Symbolic Instruction Code
bat., batt.   **1.** battalion **2.** battery
Bav.   Bavaria(n)

BAWA British Amateur Wrestling Association

BB 1. Boys' Brigade 2. double black (pencils)

bb. books

BBA 1. Bachelor of Business Administration 2. British Bankers' Association 3. British Beekeepers' Association

BBB 1. Better Business Bureau (US) 2. triple black (pencils)

BBBC British Boxing Board of Control

BBC British Broadcasting Corporation

BBFC British Board of Film Censors

bbl. barrel

BBTA British Bureau of Television Advertising

BC 1. Bachelor of Chemistry 2. Bachelor of Commerce 3. Battery Commander 4. before Christ 5. Board of Control 6. British Columbia 7. British Council

BCA Bureau of Current Affairs

BCAB Birth Control Advisory Bureau

BCal British Caledonian Airways Ltd.

BCC British Council of Churches

BCD *DP* binary coded decimal notation

BCE 1. Bachelor of Chemical Engineering 2. Bachelor of Civil Engineering 3. before the Common Era 4. Board of Customs and Excise

BCF 1. British Chess Federation
2. British Cycling Federation
BCG Bacillus Calmette-Guérin, anti-tuberculosis vaccine
BCh 1. *Baccalaureus Chirurgiae* (L. Bachelor of Surgery) 2. Bachelor of Chemistry
bch. bunch
BChD Bachelor of Dental Surgery
BChE Bachelor of Chemical Engineering
BCL 1. Bachelor of Canon Law
2. Bachelor of Civil Law
BComm Bachelor of Commerce
BCPA British Copyright Protection Association
BCS 1. Bachelor of Chemical Science
2. British Cardiac Society 3. British Cartographic Society 4. British Computer Society
BCSO British Commonwealth Scientific Office
BD 1. Bachelor of Divinity 2. bills discounted
B/D bank draft
bd. 1. board 2. bond 3. bound 4. bundle
b/d 1. barrels per day 2. brought down
BDA 1. British Dental Association
2. British Diabetic Association
BDC Book Development Council

Bde. Brigade
bd. ft. board foot
bdl. bundle
BDS 1. Bachelor of Dental Surgery
 2. *IVR* Barbados
bds. (bound in) boards
BDSc Bachelor of Dental Science
BDU Bomb Disposal Unit
BE 1. Bachelor of Economics 2. Bachelor
 of Education 3. Bank of England 4. Bill of
 Exchange 5. Board of Education
 6. British Embassy
Be *Chem.* beryllium
BEA 1. British Epilepsy Association
 2. British European Airways
BEAB British Electrical Approvals Board
BEAMA British Electrical and Allied
 Manufacturers' Association
bec. because
BEcon Bachelor of Economics'
BEconIA Bachelor of Economics in
 Industrial Administration
BEconPA Bachelor of Economics in
 Public Administration
BEd Bachelor of Education
Beds. Bedfordshire
BEE Bachelor of Electrical Engineering
BEF British Expeditionary Force
bef. before
beg. begin(ning)

Belg. **1.** Belgian **2.** Belgic **3.** Belgium
BEM British Empire Medal
BEMB British Egg Marketing Board
BEng Bachelor of Engineering
Beng. Bengal(i)
BEngSc Bachelor of Engineering Science
beq. bequeath(ed)
beqt. bequest
Berks. Berkshire
BES British Ecological Society
bet. between
BeV billion electron-volts
BF **1.** Bachelor of Finance **2.** Bachelor of Forestry
B/F brought forward
b.f. **1.** bloody fool **2.** *Ptg.* bold face **3.** *bona fide* (*L.* genuinely)
BFA Bachelor of Fine Arts
BFAMus Bachelor of Fine Arts in Music
BFBS **1.** British and Foreign Bible Society **2.** British Forces Broadcasting Service
BFI British Film Institute
BFN British Forces Network
BFPO British Forces Post Office
BG **1.** Brigadier General **2.** *IVR* Bulgaria
bg. bag
BGA British Gliding Association
BGC British Gas Council
BH *IVR* British Honduras

BHA British Homeopathic Association
B'ham Birmingham
BHC British High Commissioner
BHI British Horological Institute
BHN Brinell hardness number
b.h.p. brake horsepower
BHRA British Hotels and Restaurants Association
BHy Bachelor of Hygiene
BI Bureau of Investigation (US)
Bi *Chem.* bismuth
BIA British Insurance Association
BIAC Business and Industry Advisory Committee to **OECD**
BIATA British Independent Air Transport Association
Bib. 1. Bible 2. Biblical
Bibl. Biblical
bibl. 1. bibliographical 2. bibliography 3. bibliotheca
bibliog. 1. bibliographer 2. bibliography
bicarb. bicarbonate of soda
BICC British Insulated Callender's Cables
BID Bachelor of Industrial Design
b.i.d. *bis in die* (*L.* twice daily)
BIE Bachelor of Industrial Engineering
BIET British Institute of Engineering Technology
BIF British Industries Fair
BILS British International Law Society

BIM   British Institute of Management

biog.   1. biographical 2. biographer
3. biography

biol.   1. biological 2. biologist 3. biology

BIR   1. Board of Inland Revenue
2. British Institute of Radiology

BIRE   British Institution of Radio
Engineers

BIS   Bank for International Settlements

bis.   bissextile

BISF   British Iron and Steel Federation

BIT   1. Bachelor of Industrial Technology
2. *DP* bi*nary dig*it

BJ   Bachelor of Journalism

BJur   Bachelor of Jurisprudence

Bk   *Chem.* berkelium

bk.   1. bank 2. bark 3. block 4. book
5. break

bkcy.   bankruptcy

bkg.   banking

bkpt.   bankrupt

bks.   barracks

bkt.   1. basket 2. bracket

BL   1. Bachelor of Laws 2. Bachelor of
Letters 3. British Legion (now **RBL**)
4. British Leyland 5. British Library

B/L   Bill of Lading

bl.   1. bale 2. barrel 3. black 4. blue

BLA   British Legal Association

bldg.   building

BLit   Bachelor of Literature
BLitt   *Baccalaureus Literarum* (*L.*
Bachelor of Letters)
blk.   1. black 2. block 3. bulk
B.LL.   Bachelor of Laws
BLS   1. Bachelor in Library Science
2. Bureau of Labor Statistics (US)
blvd.   boulevard
BM   1. Bachelor of Medicine 2. *Beatae
Memoriae* (*L.* of blessed memory)
3. bench mark 4. bowel movement
5. Brigade Major 6. British Museum
b.m.   board measure
BMA   British Medical Association
BMarE   Bachelor of Marine Engineering
BMC   British Medical Council
BME   Bachelor of Mining Engineering
BMechE   Bachelor of Mechanical
Engineering
BMEF   British Mechanical Engineering
Federation
BMet   Bachelor of Metallurgy
BMEWS (bē myōōz')   ballistic missile
early warning system (US)
BMJ   British Medical Journal
BML   1. Bachelor of Modern Languages
2. British Museum Library
BMR   basal metabolic rate
BMus   Bachelor of Music
BN   bank note

Bn. **1.** Baron **2.** Battalion
BNA British Nursing Association
BNC Brasenose College, Oxford
BNOC British National Oil Corporation
BO **1.** Back Order **2.** body odour **3.** Box
Office **4.** Branch Office **5.** Broker's
Order **6.** Buyer's Option
b/o brought over
BOA **1.** British Olympic Association
2. British Optical Association **3.** British
Orthopaedic Association **4.** British
Osteopathic Association
BOAC British Overseas Airways
Corporation
BOC British Oxygen Company
BOD biochemical oxygen demand
BOE Board of Education
BOF basic oxygen furnace
Boh. Bohemia(n)
Bol. Bolivia(n)
bor. borough
BOS basic oxygen steelmaking
BOT Board of Trade
bot. **1.** botanical **2.** botanist **3.** botany
4. bottle **5.** bought
boul. boulevard
BP **1.** Bachelor of Pharmacy **2.** British
Petroleum **3.** British Pharmacopoeia
4. British Public
b/p **1.** bills payable **2.** blueprint

bp. 1. baptised 2. birthplace 3. bishop
b.p. 1. below proof 2. bill of parcels 3. boiling point
BPA 1. British Paediatric Assoication 2. British Philatelic Association
BPC British Pharmaceutical Codex
b.p.d. barrels per day
BPE Bachelor of Physical Education
BPh, BPhil Bachelor of Philosophy
BPharm Bachelor of Pharmacy
bpl. birthplace
BPOE Benevolent and Protective Order of Elks (US)
BPS 1. British Pharmacological Society 2. British Phrenological Society 3. British Printing Society 4. British Psychological Society
BQ *bene quiescat* (*L.* may he/she rest well)
bque. barque
BR 1. *IVR* Brazil 2. British Rail
B/R bills receivable
Br *Chem.* bromine
Br. 1. Breton 2. Britain 3. British 4. Brother
br. 1. branch 2. brand 3. brig 4. bronze 5. brother 6. brown
Braz. Brazil(ian)
BRC British Research Council
BRCS British Red Cross Society

BRDC   British Research and Development Corporation

brev.   brevet(ed)

Brig.   **1.** Brigade **2.** Brigadier

Brig. Gen.   Brigadier General

Brit.   **1.** Britain **2.** Britannia **3.** British **4.** Briton

BRN   *IVR* Bahrain

bro.   brother

BRS   British Road Services

BRU   *IVR* Brunei

BS   **1.** Bachelor of Science **2.** Bachelor of Surgery **3.** *IVR* Bahamas **4.** Balance Sheet **5.** Bill of Sale **6.** Blessed Sacrament **7.** British Standards

b.s.   **1.** balance sheet **2.** bill of sale

BSA   **1.** Bachelor of Science in Agriculture **2.** Birmingham Small Arms **3.** Boy Scouts of America **4.** British School of Archaeology **5.** Building Societies' Association

BSAA   Bachelor of Science in Applied Arts

BSAdv   Bachelor of Science in Advertising

BSAE   **1.** Bachelor of Science in Aeronautical Engineering **2.** Bachelor of Science in Agricultural Engineering **3.** Bachelor of Science in Architectural Engineering

BSAeE   Bachelor of Science in Aeronautical Engineering

BSAgE   Bachelor of Science in
Agricultural Engineering
BSAgr   Bachelor of Science in Agriculture
BSArch   Bachelor of Science in
Architecture
BSArchE   Bachelor of Science in
Architectural Engineering
BSBA   Bachelor of Science in Business
Administration
BSC   1. Bachelor of Science in Commerce
2. British Safety Council   3. British Society
of Commerce   4. British Steel Corporation
5. British Sugar Corporation
BSc   *Baccalaureus Scientiae* (*L.* Bachelor
of Science)
BScApp   Bachelor of Applied Science
BScD   Bachelor of Science in Dentistry
BSCE   Bachelor of Science in Civil
Engineering
BSCh   Bachelor of Science in Chemistry
BSChE   Bachelor of Science in Chemical
Engineering
BSCom   Bachelor of Science in
Communications
BSD   Bachelor of Science in Design
BSE   Bachelor of Science in Engineering
(US)
BSEd   Bachelor of Science in Education
BSEE   Bachelor of Science in Electrical
Engineering

BSEM Bachelor of Science in Engineering of Mines
BSEP Bachelor of Science in Engineering Physics
BSES Bachelor of Science in Engineering Sciences
BSF Bachelor of Science in Forestry
BSFS Bachelor of Science in Foreign Service
BSFT Bachelor of Science in Fuel Technology
BSG British Standard Gauge
BSHA Bachelor of Science in Hospital Administration
BSHE Bachelor of Science in Home Economics
BSHyg Bachelor of Science in Hygiene
BSI 1. British Standards Institution
2. Building Societies' Institute
BSIE Bachelor of Science in Industrial Engineering
BSIR Bachelor of Science in Industrial Relations
BSIT Bachelor of Science in Industrial Technology
BSJ Bachelor of Science in Journalism
bskt. basket
BSL 1. Bachelor of Sacred Literature
2. Bachelor of Science in Law 3. Bachelor of Science in Linguistics

BSLS Bachelor of Science in Library Science

BSM 1. Bachelor of Science in Medicine 2. Bachelor of Science in Music 3. Battery Sergeant-Major 4. British School of Motoring

BSME 1. Bachelor of Science in Mechanical Engineering 2. Bachelor of Science in Mining Engineering

BSMet Bachelor of Science in Metallurgy

BSMin Bachelor of Science in Mineralogy

BSMT Bachelor of Science in Medical Technology

BSNA Bachelor of Science in Nursing Administration

BSOT Bachelor of Science in Occupational Therapy

BSP Bachelor of Science in Pharmacy

BSPA Bachelor of Science in Public Administration

BSPH Bachelor of Science in Public Health

BSS British Standards Specification

BSSA Bachelor of Science in Secretarial Administration

BSSS 1. Bachelor of Science in Secretarial Studies 2. Bachelor of Science in Social Science

BST 1. British Standard Time 2. British Summer Time

BT   Bachelor of Theology
Bt.   Baronet
BTA   **1.** Blood Transfusion Association
  (US) **2.** British Travel Association
BTC   British Transport Commission
BTh   Bachelor of Theology
BThU   British thermal unit
btl.   bottle
btry.   battery
BTU   Board of Trade Unit
Btu   British thermal unit
bu.   **1.** bureau **2.** bushel
BUA   British United Airways
Bucks.   Buckinghamshire
bul.   bulletin
Bulg.   Bulgaria(n)
bull.   bulletin
BUP   British United Press
BUPA (byōō′pə)   British United Provident
  Association
BUR   *IVR* Burma
Bur.   **1.** Burma **2.** Burmese
bur.   bureau
bus.   business
BV   **1.** *beata virgo* (*L.* Blessed Virgin)
  2. *bene vale* (*L.* farewell)
BVA   British Veterinary Association
BVJ   British Veterinary Journal
BVMS   Bachelor of Veterinary Medicine
  and Surgery

bvt. brevet(ed)
b/w black and white
BWB British Waterways Board
BWI British West Indies
BWTA British Womens' Temperance
Association
BX base exchange
bx. box(es)
Byz. Byzantine
Bz *Chem.* benzene

C

C 1. Caesar 2. Canon 3. *Phys.*
capacitance 4. Cape 5. Captain
6. *Chem.* carbon 7. Catechism
8. Catholic 9. Celsius 10. Celtic
11. Centigrade 12. Central 13. Century
14. Chancellor 15. Chancery
16. Chapter 17. Chief 18. Church
19. Circuit 20. Collected
21. Commander 22. Confessor
23. Confidential 24. Congregational
25. Congress 26. Conservative
27. Constable 28. Consul 29. Contralto
30. Contrast 31. Corps 32. coulomb
33. Count 34. County 35. Court

36. Cruiser **37.** *IVR* Cuba **38.** Cubic **39.** *Phys.* heat capacity **40.** *Roman numeral for* 100

c. **1.** candle **2.** canon **3.** carat **4.** case **5.** catcher **6.** cathode **7.** caught **8.** cent **9.** centavo **10.** centigramme **11.** centime **12.** centimetre **13.** central **14.** centre **15.** *centum* **16.** century **17.** chapter **18.** charge **19.** *circa* (*L.* about) **20.** city **21.** class **22.** college **23.** *Math.* constant **24.** contralto **25.** copyright **26.** cubic **27.** cup **28.** currency **29.** current **30.** cycle **31.** *Phys.* specific heat capacity

CA **1.** Caterers' Association of Great Britain **2.** Central America **3.** Chartered Accountant **4.** Chief Accountant **5.** Chronological Age **6.** Church Assembly **7.** Civil Aviation **8.** College of Arms **9.** Commercial Agent **10.** Companies Act **11.** Confederate Army **12.** Consular Agent **13.** Consumers' Association **14.** Controller of Accounts **15.** Court of Appeal **16.** Crown Agent **17.** Member of the Institute of Chartered Accountants of Scotland

C/A **1.** Capital Account **2.** Credit Account **3.** Current Account

Ca *Chem.* calcium

ca. 1. case 2. cathode 3. centiare 4. *circa* (*L.* about)...

CAA 1. Canadian Authors' Association 2. Civil Aeronautics Administration 3. Civil Aviation Authority 4. Cost Accountants Association

CAAA Canadian Association of Advertising Agencies

CAAE Canadian Association for Adult Education

CAB 1. Canadian Association of Broadcasters 2. Citizens' Advice Bureau 3. Civil Aeronautics Board (US) 4. Commonwealth Agricultural Bureaux

CAC 1. Central Advisory Committee 2. Consumers' Advisory Council (US)

CACCI Confederation of Asian Chambers of Commerce and Industry

CAD Civil Air Defense (US)

cad. *Mus.* cadenza (*It.* final flourish)

c.a.d. cash against documents

CADF Commutated Antenna Direction Finder

CAE 1. Canadian Aviation Electronics 2. Chartered Automobile Engineer

CAEA Central American Economics Association

CAEAI Chartered Auctioneers' and Estate Agents' Institute

Caern. Caernarvonshire (former county)

CAES   Canadian Agricultural Economics Society

CAF   cost and freight

CAFTA (kaf'tə)   Central American Free Trade Association

CAG   1. Canadian Association of Geographers   2. Civil Air Guard (US)

CAI   1. Canadian Aeronautical Institute   2. *DP* computer-assisted instruction

CAIB   Certified Associate of the Institute of Bankers

Caith.   Caithness (former county)

Cal.   1. Calcutta   2. Caledonia   3. California

cal.   1. calendar   2. calibre   3. calorie

CALPA (kal'pə)   Canadian Air Line Pilots' Association

Cambs.   Cambridgeshire

CAN   Customs assigned number

Can.   1. Canada   2. Canadian   3. Canberra   4. Canon   5. Canto

can.   1. canal   2. cancel   3. cannon   4. canton

Canad.   Canadian

canc.   1. cancellation   2. cancelled

cand.   candidate

c & b   *Cricket* caught and bowled

c & d   collection and delivery

c & f   cost and freight

C & W   *Mus.* country and western

Cant. 1. Canterbury 2. Canticles
3. Cantonese

Cantab. *Cantabrigiensis* (*L.* of
Cambridge)

Cantaur. *Cantaurensis* (*L.* of
Canterbury)

CAP 1. Canadian Association of
Physicists 2. Civil Air Patrol (US)
3. Code of Advertising Practice
4. Common Agricultural Policy (of **EEC**)

cap. 1. capacity 2. capital 3. capitalize
4. captain 5. *caput* (*L.* chapter)

CAPAC Composers', Authors' and
Publishers' Association of Canada

caps. 1. capital letters 2. capsule

Capt. Captain

CAR 1. Canadian Association of
Radiologists 2. Central African Republic
3. Civil Air Regulations

car. carat

CARD Campaign Against Racial
Discrimination

Card. 1. Cardiganshire (former county)
2. Cardinal

CARDE Canadian Armament Research
and Development Establishment

CARE (kãər) Cooperative for American
Relief Everywhere

Carms. Carmarthenshire (former county)

carp. 1. carpenter 2. carpentry

carr. carriage
cartog. cartography
cas. 1. casual 2. casualty
CASA Canadian Amateur Swimming Association
CA(SA) Member of the Accountants' Society (South Africa)
cash. cashier
CASI Canadian Aeronautics and Space Institute
CAT 1. Civil Air Transport 2. clear air turbulence 3. (kat) College of Advanced Technology
cat. 1. catalogue 2. catamaran 3. catapult 4. catechism
CATC Commonwealth Air Transport Commission
Cath. 1. Cathedral 2. Catholic
cath. cathode
CATV Community Antenna Television (US)
caus. 1. causation 2. causative
cav. 1. cavalier 2. cavalry
CAVU *Aeron.* ceiling and visibility unlimited
CAWU Clerical and Administrative Workers' Union
CAX *DP* community automatic exchange
CB 1. Cape Breton 2. Cash Book 3. *Radio* Citizens' Band 4. Companion of

the Order of the Bath **5.** *Mil.* confinement
to barracks **6.** County Borough
Cb *Chem.* columbium
CBA Council for British Archaeology
CBAE Commonwealth Bureau of
Agricultural Economics
CBC Canadian Broadcasting Corporation
c.b.d. cash before delivery
CBE Commander of the Order of the
British Empire
CBF Central Board of Finance
CBI **1.** Central Bureau of Investigation
(US) **2.** Confederation of British Industry
CBPC Canadian Book Publishers' Council
CBS **1.** Columbia Broadcasting System
2. Confraternity of the Blessed Sacrament
CBW chemical and biological warfare
CC **1.** carbon copy **2.** Cashier's Check
(US) **3.** Chamber of Commerce **4.** Chief
Clerk **5.** Circuit Court **6.** City Council
7. Civil Court **8.** closed circuit
9. Companion of the Order of Canada
10. County Council **11.** County Court
12. Credit Card **13.** Cricket Club
Cc *Met.* cirrocumulus
cc cubic centimetre(s)
cc. **1.** centuries **2.** chapters **3.** copies
CCA **1.** Canadian Chemical Association
2. Canadian Construction Association
3. Circuit Court of Appeals (US)

4. Commonwealth Correspondents' Association

CCC **1.** Canadian Chamber of Commerce **2.** Central Criminal Court **3.** Civilian Conservation Corps (US) **4.** Commodity Credit Corporation (US) **5.** Corpus Christi College **6.** County Cricket Club

CCCP *Soyuz Sovietskikh Sotsialisticheskikh Respublik* (*Russ.* Union of Soviet Socialist Republics)

CCF **1.** Combined Cadet Force **2.** Cooperative Commonwealth Federation (Can.)

CCFA Combined Cadet Force Association

CCHE Central Council for Health Education

CChem Chartered Chemist

CCHR Citizens' Commission on Human Rights

CCJ Circuit *or* County Court Judge

CCP **1.** Chinese Communist Party **2.** Code of Civil Procedure **3.** Court of Common Pleas

CCR Commission on Civil Rights (US)

CCS **1.** Canadian Cancer Society **2.** Casualty Clearing Station **3.** Corporation of Certified Secretaries

CCTV closed circuit television

CCUS Chamber of Commerce of the United States

c.c.w. counter-clockwise
CD 1. Canadian Forces Decoration
2. Chancery Division 3. Civil Defence
4. contagious disease 5. Corps
Diplomatique
C/D 1. Certificate of Deposit
2. Customs Declaration
Cd *Chem.* cadmium
cd candela
cd. 1. cord 2. could
c.d. cash discount
c/d carried down
CDA 1. Canadian Dental Association
2. Civil Defence Act
cdbd. cardboard
CDC Commonwealth Development
Corporation
CDEE Chemical Defence Experimental
Establishment
CDN *IVR* Canada
Cdr. 1. Commander 2. Conductor
Cdre. Commodore
CDS 1. Chief of the Defence Staff
2. Civil Defence Services
CDSO Companion of the Distinguished
Service Order
CDT Central Daylight Time (US)
Cdt. 1. Cadet 2. Commandant
CDU Christian Democratic Union
CDV Civil Defence Volunteers

CE **1.** Chancellor of the Exchequer **2.** Chemical Engineer **3.** Chief Engineer **4.** Christian Endeavour **5.** Church of England **6.** Civil Engineer **7.** Common Era **8.** Council of Europe

Ce *Chem.* cerium

CEA **1.** Canadian Electrical Association **2.** Central Electrical Authority **3.** Council of Economic Advisers (US)

CEB Central Electricity Board

CEC **1.** Civil Engineering Corps **2.** Commonwealth Economic Committee

CED Committee for Economic Development (US)

CEDA Committee for the Economic Development of Australia

CEDO Centre for Educational Development Overseas

CEEC Council for European Economic Cooperation

CEF Canadian Expeditionary Force

CEGB Central Electricity Generating Board

CEI Council of Engineering Institutions

Cel. Celsius

cel. **1.** celebrated **2.** celibate

Celt. Celtic

Cem. Cemetery

CEMA Council for the Encouragement of Music and the Arts (now **ACGB**)

cen. 1. central 2. centre 3. century
CEng Chartered Engineer
cent. 1. centavo 2. centigrade
 3. centime 4. centimetre 5. central
 6. *centum* (*L.* a hundred) 7. century
CENTO (sen′tō) Central Treaty
 Organization
CEO 1. Chief Education Officer 2. Chief
 Executive Officer
cer. ceramics
CERA Civil Engineering Research
 Association
CERL Central Electricity Research
 Laboratories
CERN *Conseil Européen pour la
 Recherche Nucléaire* (*Fr.* European
 Organization for Nuclear Research)
cert. 1. certain 2. certificate
 3. certification 4. certified 5. certify
CertAIB Certificated Associate of the
 Institute of Bankers
CertEd Certificate in Education
CESA Canadian Engineering Standards
 Association
Cestr. *Cestrensis* (*L.* of Chester)
CET Central European Time
cet. par. *ceteris paribus* (*L.* other things
 being equal)
CETS Church of England Temperance
 Society

CF **1.** Chaplain to the Forces **2.** Commonwealth Fund **3.** cost and freight

Cf *Chem.* californium

cf. **1.** calf **2.** *confer* (*L.* compare)

c/f carried forward

CFA **1.** Canadian Federation of Agriculture **2.** Canadian Forestry Association **3.** Certified Financial Analyst (US) **4.** Commonwealth Forestry Association

CFI cost, freight and insurance

CFM **1.** Cadet Forces Medal **2.** Council of Foreign Ministers

cfm cubic feet per minute

cfs cubic feet per second

cft cubic foot *or* feet

CG **1.** Coast Guard **2.** Coldstream Guards **3.** Commanding General **4.** Consul General

cg centigram

c.g. centre of gravity

CGA Canadian Gas Association

CGH Cape of Good Hope

CGI City and Guilds Institute

c.g.i. corrugated galvanized iron

CGIA City and Guilds of London Insignia Award

CGLI City and Guilds of London Institute

CGM Conspicuous Gallantry Medal

cgm   centigram
CGS   Chief of the General Staff
cgs   centimetre-gram-second
CGT   Capital Gains Tax
CH   1. Companion of Honour 2. Court House 3. Custom House 4. *IVR* Switzerland
Ch.   1. Chairman 2. Chaldean 3. Chaldee 4. China 5. Chinese
ch.   1. chain 2. champion 3. chaplain 4. chapter 5. check 6. chemical 7. chemistry 8. chief 9. child 10. choir 11. church
c.h.   central heating
Chal.   1. Chaldaic 2. Chaldee
Chamb.   Chamberlain
chan.   channel
Chanc.   1. Chancellor 2. Chancery
Chap.   1. Chapel 2. Chaplain
chap.   chapter
char.   1. character 2. charity 3. charter
ChB   *Chirurgiae Baccalaureus* (*L.* Bachelor of Surgery)
Ch. Ch.   Christ Church, Oxford
CHD   coronary heart disease
ChD   1. Chancery Division 2. Doctor of Chemistry
ChE   Chemical Engineer
chem.   1. chemical 2. chemist 3. chemistry

Ches.   Cheshire
chg.   1. change 2. charge
chgd.   charged
Ch. Hist.   Church History
Chin.   1. China 2. Chinese
ChJ   Chief Justice
ChM   *Chirurgiae Magister* (*L.* Master of Surgery)
Chm.   1. Chairman 2. checkmate
chq.   cheque
Chr.   1. Christ 2. Christian 3. Chronicles
Chron.   *Bib.* Chronicles
chron.   1. chronicle 2. chronological 3. chronology 4. chronometry
chs.   chapters
CI   1. Channel Islands 2. Commonwealth Institute 3. Imperial Order of the Crown of India 4. *IVR* Ivory Coast
Ci.   1. cirrus 2. curie
CIA   1. Central Intelligence Agency (US) 2. Chemical Industries Association 3. Commonwealth Industries Association
CIB   Corporation of Insurance Brokers
CIC   1. Chemical Institute of Canada 2. Counter Intelligence Corps (US)
CICA   Canadian Institute of Chartered Accountants
Cicestr.   *Cicestrensis* (*L.* of Chichester)

CID

CID   **1.** Council of Industrial Design
   2. Criminal Investigation Department
CIE   **1.** Companion of the Order of the
   Indian Empire **2.** *Coras Iompair Eireann*
   (*Gael.* Transport Organization of Ireland)
CIEE   Companion of the Institution of
Electrical Engineers
CIF, cif   cost, insurance and freight
CIGS   Chief of the Imperial General Staff
CII   **1.** Chartered Insurance Institute
   2. Confederation of Irish Industry
CIIA   Canadian Institute of International
Affairs
CIM   **1.** Canadian Institute of Mining
   2. Commission on Industry and Manpower
CIMarE   Companion of the Institute of
Marine Engineers
CIMechE   Companion of the Institution of
Mechanical Engineers
CIMM   Canadian Institute of Mining and
Metallurgy
C-in-C   Commander-in-Chief
Cinn.   Cincinnati
CIO   Congress of Industrial Organizations
(US)
CIPA   Chartered Institute of Patent Agents
CIR   Commission on Industrial Relations
cir.   **1.** *circa* (*L.* about) **2.** circle
   3. circuit **4.** circular **5.** circulation
   6. circumference

CIS   **1.** Chartered Institute of Secretaries **2.** Counter Information Services

cit.   **1.** citadel **2.** citation **3.** cited **4.** citizen **5.** citrate

CITB   Construction Industry Training Board

civ.   **1.** civil **2.** civilian **3.** civilization

CJ   Chief Justice

CJCC   Commonwealth Joint Communications Committee

ck.   **1.** cask **2.** check (US)

ckw.   clockwise

CL   **1.** Civil Law **2.** *IVR* Sri Lanka

Cl   *Chem.* chlorine

cl   centilitre

cl.   **1.** claim **2.** class **3.** classical **4.** classification **5.** clause **6.** clearance **7.** clergyman **8.** clerk **9.** cloth

c.l.   **1.** carload **2.** centre line **3.** civil law

CLA   Canadian Library Association

clar.   clarinet

class.   **1.** classic **2.** classical **3.** classification **4.** classified

CLD   Doctor of Civil Law

cld.   **1.** called **2.** cancelled **3.** cleared **4.** coloured **5.** could

cler.   clerical

clin.   clinical

CLitt   Companion of Literature

clk.   **1.** clerk **2.** clock

Cllr. Councillor
CLR Computer Language Recorder
CLT Computer Language Translator
CLU 1. Chartered Life Underwriter
2. Civil Liberties Union
CM 1. Canada Medal 2. Certificated
Master 3. Chief Minister 4. *Chirurgiae
Magister* (*L.* Master of Surgery)
5. Corresponding Member
Cm *Chem.* curium
cm centimetre
c.m. 1. *carat métrique* (*Fr.* metric carat)
2. *causa mortis* (*L.* in case of or by reason
of death) 3. circular mail 4. common
metre 5. corresponding
member 6. countermarked 7. court
martial
CMA Canadian Medical Association
cmd. command
cmdg. commanding
Cmdr. Commander
Cmdre. Commodore
Cmdt. Commandant
CMEA Council for Mutual Economic
Assistance
CMET Council on Middle East Trade
CMF Commonwealth Military Force
CMG 1. Companion of the Order of St
Michael and St George 2. Congress Medal
for Gallantry (US)

CMH Congressional Medal of Honor (US)
cml. commercial
CMO Chief Medical Officer
CMRST Committee on Manpower Resources for Science and Technology
CMS Church Missionary Society
CN chloroacetophenone
C/N 1. Circular Note 2. Cover Note 3. Credit Note
CNAA Council for National Academic Awards
CNAS Chief of Naval Air Services
CND Campaign for Nuclear Disarmament
CNI Chief of Naval Information
CNIB Canadian National Institute for the Blind
CNL 1. Canadian National Library 2. Commonwealth National Library, Australia
CNO Chief of Naval Operations
CNP Chief of Naval Personnel
CNR Canadian National Railways
cnr. corner
CNS 1. central nervous system 2. Chief of Naval Staff
CO 1. Cash Order 2. *IVR* Colombia 3. Commanding Officer 4. conscientious objector 5. Criminal Office 6. Crown Office
Co *Chem.* cobalt

Co. 1. Commerce 2. Company
3. County

c/o 1. care of 2. carried over

coad. coadjutor

Coal. Coalition

COBOL (kō'bol) *DP* common business oriented language

COD 1. cash on delivery 2. collect on delivery (US)

Cod. Codex

cod. 1. codicil 2. codification

coef. coefficient

C of A 1. Certificate of Airworthiness 2. College of Arms

C of C Chamber of Commerce

C of E 1. Church of England 2. Council of Europe

C of I Church of Ireland

C of S 1. Chief of Staff 2. Church of Scotland

cog. 1. cognate 2. cognisant

c.o.g. centre of gravity

COGB Certified Official Government Business

c.o.h. cash on hand

COHSE (kō'zē) Confederation of Health Service Employees

COI Central Office of Information

COID Council of Industrial Design

COL computer-oriented language

Col. 1. Colonel 2. Colorado 3. *Bib.*
Colossians 4. Columbia(n)

col. 1. collected 2. collector 3. college
4. colonial 5. colony 6. colour
7. coloured 8. column

coll. 1. collateral 2. colleague
3. collection 4. collector 5. college
6. collegiate 7. colloquial

collab. 1. collaborate 2. collaboration
3. collaborator

collat. collateral

colloq. 1. colloquial 2. colloquialism
3. colloquially

Colo. Colorado

Coloss. *Bib.* Colossians

COM computer-output microfilm

Com. 1. Commander 2. Commerce
3. Commission 4. Commissioner
5. Committee 6. Commodore
7. Commonwealth 8. Communist

com. 1. comedy 2. comic 3. comma
4. commerce 5. commercial
6. committee 7. common(ly)
8. communication 9. community

comb. 1. combination 2. combining
3. combustible

Comdt. Commandant

COMECON (kom′i kon′) Council for
Mutual Economic Aid

COMEXO (ko mek′sō) Committee for
Oceanic Exploration
comm. 1. commander 2. commentary
 3. commerce 4. commercial
 5. commissary 6. commission
 7. committee 8. commonwealth
 9. communication
Commissr. Commissioner
commn. commission
Commy. Commissary
comp. 1. companion 2. comparative
 3. compare 4. comparison
 5. compensation 6. competitor
 7. compiled 8. compilation 9. complete
 10. composer 11. composition
 12. compositor 13. compound
 14. comprehensive 15. comprising
compar. 1. comparative 2. comparison
compd. compound
compl. 1. complement 2. complete
 3. compliment(ary)
Comr. Commissioner
COMSAT (kom′sat) Communications
Satellite (US)
Com. Ver. Common Version (of the
Bible)
Con. 1. Conformist 2. Consul
con. 1. concentration 2. concerning
 3. concerto 4. conclusion 5. *conjunx* (*L.*
wife) 6. connection 7. consolidated

8. consort 9. consul 10. continued
11. *contra* (*L.* against) 12. convenience
13. conversation

conc. 1. concentrate(d)
2. concentration 3. concerning

conch. conchology

cond. 1. condenser 2. conditional
3. conducted 4. conductivity
5. conductor

conf. 1. *confer* (*L.* compare)
2. conference 3. confessor

Confed. 1. Confederate
2. Confederation

Cong. 1. Congregational
2. Congress(ional)

cong. 1. *congius* (*L.* gallon)
2. congregation

conj. 1. conjugation 2. conjunction
3. conjunctive

Conn. Connecticut

conn. 1. connected 2. connection
3. connotation

Cons. 1. Conservative 2. Constable
3. Constitution 4. Consul

cons. 1. consecrated 2. consecutive
3. consequence 4. consigned
5. consignment 6. consolidated
7. consonant 8. constitution
9. construction 10. consulting

con. sec. conic section

Consols Consolidated Funds
const. 1. constable 2. constant
   3. constitution
constr. 1. construction 2. construed
Cont. Continental
cont. 1. containing 2. contents
   3. continent(al) 4. continued 5. *contra*
   (*L.* against) 6. contract 7. control
contd. 1. contained 2. continued
contemp. contemporary
contg. containing
contr. 1. contract 2. contraction
   3. contralto 4. contrary 5. contrast
   6. control(ler)
contrib. 1. contribution 2. contributor
conv. 1. convenient 2. conventional
   3. conversation
co-op co-operative
Cop. Coptic
COPE Committee on Political Education
   (US)
COPEC (kō'pek) Conference on Politics,
   Economics and Christianity
Cor. 1. *Bib.* Corinthians 2. Coroner
   3. Corsica
cor. 1. corner 2. cornet 3. coroner
   4. *corpus* (*L.* the body) 5. correct(ion)
   6. correlative 7. correspondence
   8. corresponding

CORE (kôr)   Congress of Racial Equality (US)

corol.   corollary

Corp.   1. Corporal 2. Corporation

corpl.   corporal

corpn.   corporation

corr.   1. correct(ion) 2. correspondence 3. corresponding 4. corrugated 5. corruption

correl.   correlative

COS   1. cash on shipment 2. Chief of Staff

cos   *Math.* cosine

COSE   Committee on Secondary Education (Scotland)

cosec   *Math.* cosecant

cosech   *Math.* hyperbolic cosecant

cosh   *Math.* hyperbolic cosine

cosmog.   cosmography

COSPAR (kos'pär)   Committee on Space Research

cot, cotan   *Math.* cotangent

COTC   Canadian Overseas Telecommunications Corporation

coth   *Math.* hyperbolic cotangent

covers   *Math.* coversed sine

Cox.   Coxswain

Coy.   *Mil.* Company

CP   1. Cape Province 2. Carriage Paid 3. Chief Patriarch 4. Clerk of the Peace

5. College of Preceptors **6.** Command Post **7.** Common Pleas **8.** Common Prayer **9.** Communist Party **10.** Country Party (Aust.) **11.** Court of Probate

cp. compare

c.p. 1. candle power **2.** chemically pure

CPA 1. Canadian Pacific Airlines
2. Canadian Pharmaceutical Association
3. Canadian Postmasters' Association
4. Canadian Psychological Association
5. Certified Public Accountant (US)
6. Chartered Patent Agent
7. Commonwealth Parliamentary Association

CPAG Child Poverty Action Group

CPC 1. Christian Peace Conference
2. Clerk of the Privy Council

CPCU Chartered Property and Casualty Underwriter (US)

cpd. compound

CPHA Canadian Public Health Association

CPI 1. characters per inch **2.** consumer price index

Cpl. Corporal

CPM *DP* critical path method

cpm cycles per minute

CPO 1. Chief Petty Officer
2. Commonwealth Producers' Organization

CPR Canadian Pacific Railway

CPRE Council for the Preservation of Rural England

CPRI Canadian Peace Research Institute

CPRW Council for the Preservation of Rural Wales

CPS *Custos Privati Sigilli* (*L.* Keeper of the Privy Seal)

cps 1. characters per second 2. cycles per second

CPSA 1. Canadian Political Science Association 2. Civil and Public Services Association

CPSU Communist Party of the Soviet Union

cpt. counterpoint

CPU 1. *DP* central processing unit 2. Commonwealth Press Union

CQ 1. *Radio* call to quarters 2. *Mil.* charge of quarters

CR 1. *Carolus Rex* (*L.* King Charles) 2. *civis romanus* (*L.* Roman citizen) 3. Community of the Resurrection 4. *IVR* Costa Rica 5. *Custos Rotulorum* (*L.* Keeper of the Rolls)

Cr *Chem.* chromium

Cr. 1. Councillor 2. Creditor

cr. 1. credit(or) 2. crown

CRAC Careers Research and Advisory Centre

CRCC Canadian Red Cross Committee

CRD chronic respiratory disease
CRE Commission for Racial Equality
Cres. Crescent
cres. *Mus. crescendo* (*It.* increasing)
crim. criminal
crim. con. *Law* criminal conversation, ie adultery
crit. 1. criterion 2. critical 3. criticism 4. criticize
CRMP Corps of Royal Military Police
CRO 1. cathode-ray oscillograph 2. Commonwealth Relations Office 3. Criminal Records Office
crs. 1. creditors 2. credits
CRT cathode-ray tube
cryst. 1. crystalline 2. crystallized 3. crystallography
CS 1. Capital Stock 2. Chartered Surveyor 3. Chemical Society 4. Christian Science 5. Civil Service 6. Clerk of Session 7. Clerk to the Signet 8. Confederate States 9. Court of Session 10. *IVR* Czechoslovakia
Cs 1. *Chem.* caesium 2. *Met.* cirrostratus
cs. case
CSA 1. Canadian Standards Association 2. Confederate States of America
CSC 1. Civil Service Commission 2. Conspicuous Service Cross (now **DSC**)

csc *Math.* cosecant

csch *Math.* hyperbolic cosecant

CSE Certificate of Secondary Education

CSEU Confederation of Shipbuilding and Engineering Unions

CSI 1. Chartered Surveyors' Institution 2. Companion of the Order of the Star of India

C.S.I.R.O. Commonwealth Scientific and Industrial Research Organization

csk. cask

CSLO Canadian Scientific Liaison Office

CSM Company Sergeant-Major

CSO 1. Central Statistical Office 2. Chief Signal Officer 3. Chief Staff Officer

CSP 1. Chartered Society of Physiotherapists 2. Council on Scientific Policy

CST Central Standard Time (US)

CSTI Council of Science and Technology Institutes

CSU Civil Service Union

Ct. 1. Certificate 2. Connecticut 3. Count 4. County 5. Court

ct. 1. carat 2. cent 3. *centum (L.* hundred) 4. certificate 5. county 6. court

CTA 1. Camping Trade Association 2. Commercial Travellers' Association

CTB Commonwealth Telecommunications Board

CTC Cyclists' Touring Club

ctg. cartridge

ctn *Math.* cotangent

ctr. centre

cts. 1. carats 2. centimes 3. cents

CTT Capital Transfer Tax

CU Cambridge University

Cu *Chem.* copper

Cu. *Met.* cumulus

cu. cubic

cum. cumulative

Cumb. Cumberland (former county)

CUP Cambridge University Press

CUPE Canadian Union of Public Employees

cur. 1. currency 2. current

cusec cubic feet per second

CV Curriculum Vitae

CVMA Canadian Veterinary Medical Association

CVO Commander of the Royal Victorian Order

CW *Radio* continuous wave

CWA 1. Civil Works Administration (US) 2. Crime Writers' Association

CWC 1. Catering Wages Commission 2. Commonwealth of World Citizens

Cwlth. Commonwealth

CWO   Chief Warrant Officer (US)
c.w.o.   cash with order
CWS   1. Chemical Warfare Service
2. Cooperative Wholesale Society
cwt.   hundredweight
CWU   Chemical Workers' Union
CY   *IVR* Cyprus
cy.   1. capacity 2. currency 3. cycle
cyc.   1. cycle 2. cyclopedia
3. cyclopedic
cyl.   1. cylinder 2. cylindrical
CYM   Commonwealth Youth Movement
Cym.   Cymric
CYO   Catholic Youth Organization
CZ   Canal Zone (Panama)
Czech.   Czechoslovakia(n)

D

D   1. Democratic 2. Department
3. *Deus* (*L*. God) 4. *Chem.* deuterium
5. dimension 6. diopter 7. Director
8. *Dominus* (*L*. Lord) 9. Don
10. Duchess 11. Duke 12. Dutch
13. *IVR* Germany 14. *Roman numeral for*
500
d.   1. dam 2. date 3. daughter 4. day

5. dead **6.** deceased **7.** decree
8. degree **9.** delete **10.** *denarius* (*L.*
penny) **11.** density **12.** departs
13. deputy **14.** deserter **15.** diameter
16. died **17.** dime **18.** dinar
19. diopter **20.** director **21.** dividend
22. dollar **23.** dorsal **24.** dose
25. drachma **26.** duke

DA **1.** delayed action **2.** Deposit
Account **3.** Diploma of Art **4.** District
Attorney **5.** Doctor of Arts

D/A **1.** Deposit Account **2.** Documents
for Acceptance

da. **1.** daughter **2.** day

DAB *Dictionary of American Biography*

DAE **1.** *Dictionary of American English*
2. Diploma in Advanced Engineering

DAFS Department of Agriculture and
Fisheries for Scotland

DAG Deputy Adjutant-General

dag decagram

DAgr Doctor of Agriculture

DAgrSc Doctor of Agricultural Science

Dak. Dakota

dal decalitre

dam decametre

Dan. **1.** *Bib.* Daniel **2.** Danish

D & C **1.** Dean and Chapter **2.** dilation
and curettage

D & D drunk and disorderly

DAR Daughters of the American Revolution

DArch Doctor of Architecture

DASc Doctor of Agricultural Sciences

DASM delayed action space missile

dat. dative

DATA **1.** Defense Air Transportation Administration (US) **2.** Draughtsmen's and Allied Technicians' Association

dau. daughter

DAV Disabled American Veterans

DB *Divinitatis Baccalaureus* (*L.* Bachelor of Divinity)

dB decibel

DBA Doctor of Business Administration

d.b.a. doing business as

DBE Dame Commander of the Order of the British Empire

d.b.h. diameter at breast height

D. Bib. Douay Bible

dbl. double

dbl. ch. *Chess* double check

DBM Diploma in Business Management

DBST Double British Summer Time

DC **1.** Death Certificate **2.** Depth Charge **3.** Diplomatic Corps **4.** direct current **5.** District Commissioner **6.** District of Columbia **7.** Doctor of Chiropractic

d.c. **1.** *Mus. da capo* (*It.* repeat from the

beginning) **2.** dead centre **3.** direct current **4.** double column **5.** double crochet

DCAS Deputy Chief of Air Staff

DCB **1.** Dame Commander of the Order of the Bath **2.** Decimal Currency Board

DCE **1.** Diploma in Chemical Engineering **2.** Doctor of Civil Engineering

DCh *Doctor Chirurgiae* (*L.* Doctor of Surgery)

DChE Doctor of Chemical Engineering

DChO Diploma in Ophthalmic Surgery

DCJ District Court Judge (US)

DCL Doctor of Civil Law

DClSc Doctor of Clinical Science

DCM Distinguished Conduct Medal

dcm decametre

DCMG Dame Commander of the Order of St Michael and St George

DCnL Doctor of Canon Law

DComL Doctor of Commercial Law

DComm Doctor of Commerce

DCP Diploma of Clinical Pathology

DCS **1.** Deputy Chief of Air Staff **2.** Deputy Clerk of Session **3.** Doctor of Commercial Science

DCT Doctor of Christian Tehology

dct. document

DCVO Dame Commander of the Royal Victorian Order

DD   **1.** demand draft **2.** *Deo dedit* (*L.* gave to God) **3.** direct debit **4.** *Divinitatis Doctor* (*L.* Doctor of Divinity)

dd.   **1.** dated **2.** delivered

d.d.   day's date

DDA   **1.** Dangerous Drugs Act **2.** Disabled Drivers' Association

DDC   Dewey Decimal Classification

DDD   **1.** *dat, dicat, dedicat* (*L.* gives, devotes, and dedicates) **2.** direct distance dialing (US) **3.** *dono dedit dedicavit* (*L.* gave and consecrated as a gift)

DDM   **1.** Diploma in Dermatological Medicine **2.** Doctor of Dental Medicine

DDO   Diploma in Dental Orthopaedics

DDR   *Deutsche Demokratische Republik* (German Democratic Republic)

DDS   Doctor of Dental Surgery

DDSc   Doctor of Dental Science

DDT   dichlorodiphenyltrichlorethane, an insecticide

DE   **1.** *Dáil Éirann* (lower House of Eire Parliament) **2.** Destroyer Escort **3.** Doctor of Engineering **4.** Doctor of Entomology

d.e.   double entry

Dea.   Deacon

deb.   **1.** debenture **2.** debit

Dec.   December

dec.   **1.** deceased **2.** decimal

   3. decimetre **4.** declaration
   5. declension **6.** declination **7.** decrease
   8. *Mus. decrescendo* (*It.* becoming softer)
decd. deceased
decl. **1.** declaration **2.** declension
DEcon Doctor of Economics
decresc. *decrescendo*
DEd Doctor of Education
DEE Diploma in Electrical Engineering
def. **1.** defective **2.** defence
   3. defendant **4.** deferred **5.** deficit
   6. definite **7.** definition
deg. degree
Del. Delaware
del. **1.** delegate **2.** delegation **3.** delete
Dem. Democratic
Den. Denmark
Denb. Denbighshire (former county)
DEng Doctor of Engineering
DEngS Doctor of Engineering Science
denom. denomination
dens. density
dent. **1.** dental **2.** dentist **3.** dentistry
DEP Department of Employment and
  Productivity
dep. **1.** department **2.** departs
   3. departure **4.** deponent **5.** deposed
   6. deposit **7.** depot **8.** deputy
dept. department

der., deriv. 1. derivation 2. derivative 3. derived
Derbys. Derbyshire
DERV (durv) diesel engined road vehicle
DES Department of Education and Science
desc. 1. descendant 2. describe(d)
DesRCA Designer of the Royal College of Art
Det. Detective
det. 1. detachment 2. detail
Det. Con. Detective Constable
Det. Insp. Detective Inspector
Det. Sgt. Detective Sergeant
Deut. *Bib.* Deuteronomy
dev. 1. development 2. deviation
DEW (dyoo) distant early warning
DF 1. Dean of the Faculty 2. *Defensor Fidei* (*L.* Defender of the Faith) 3. Direction Finder
DFA 1. Diploma in Foreign Affairs 2. Doctor of Fine Arts
DFC Distinguished Flying Cross
DFM 1. Diploma in Forensic Medicine 2. Distinguished Flying Medal
DFR Dounreay Fast Reactor
dft. 1. defendant 2. draft
DG 1. *Dei gratia* (*L.* by the grace of God) 2. *Deo gratias* (*L.* thanks to God)
dg decigram(me)

DGO   Diploma in Gynaecology and Obstetrics

DH   Doctor of Humanities

DHL   Doctor of Hebrew Literature

DHSS   Department of Health and Social Security

DHy   Doctor of Hygiene

DI   Defence Intelligence

di.   diameter

DIA   Diploma in International Affairs

dia.   1. diagram 2. dialect 3. diameter

diag.   1. diagonal 2. diagram

dial   1. dialect 2. dialogue

diam.   diameter

DIC   Diploma of the Imperial College

DIChem   Diploma of Industrial Chemistry

dict.   1. dictation 2. dictator 3. dictionary

DIE   1. Diploma in Industrial Engineering 2. Diploma of the Institute of Engineering

diff.   1. difference 2. different 3. differential

DIG   Disabled Income Group

dig.   1. digest 2. digit 3. digital

DIH   Diploma in Industrial Health

dil.   dilute(d)

DIM   Diploma in Industrial Management

dim.   1. dimension 2. diminished 3. *Mus.* diminuendo (*It.* becoming softer)

dimin.   1. *diminuendo* 2. diminutive

DIng   *Doctor Ingeniariae* (L. Doctor of
Engineering)
Dioc.   1. Diocesan   2. Diocese
Dip.   Diploma
DipAD   Diploma in Art and Design
DipAgr   Diploma in Agriculture
DipALing   Diploma in Applied Linguistics
DipAM   Diploma in Applied Mechanics
DipAppSc   Diploma of Applied Science
DipArch   Diploma of Architecture
DipArts   Diploma in Arts
DipBac   Diploma in Bacteriology
DipCard   Diploma in Cardiology
DipCom   Diploma of Commerce
DipEcon   Diploma of Economics
DipEd   Diploma in Education
DipEng   Diploma in Engineering
DipFA   Diploma in Fine Arts
DipHE   Diploma of Higher Education
DipJ   Diploma of Journalism
DipL   Diploma in Languages
DipLib   Diploma of Librarianship
DipLSc   Diploma of Library Science
DipMechE   Diploma of Mechanical
Engineering
DipOrth   Diploma in Orthodontics
DipPA   Diploma in Public Administration
DipPharm   Diploma in Pharmacy
DipQS   Diploma in Quantity Surveying

DipRADA   Diploma of the Royal Academy of Dramatic Art
DipSS   Diploma in Social Studies
DipT   Diploma in Teaching
DipTech   Diploma in Technology
DipTh   Diploma in Theology
Dir.   Director
dis.   1. discontinued 2. dascount 3. distance 4. distant 5. distribute
disab.   disability
disc.   1. discount 2. discovered
disch.   discharge(d)
dis. ch.   *Chess* discovered check
disp.   1. dispensary 2. dispensation 3. dispensed 4. disperse
displ.   displacement
diss.   dissertation
dist.   1. distant 2. distilled 3. distinguished 4. district
Dist. Atty.   District Attorney
distr.   1. distribute(d) 2. distribution 3. distributor
DIur   Doctor of Law
div.   1. divergence 2. divide 3. dividend 4. divine 5. division 6. divorce
DIY   do-it-yourself
DJ   1. dinner jacket 2. Diploma in Journalism 3. disc jockey
DJS   Doctor of Juridical Science

DJT   Doctor of Jewish Theology
DJur   Doctor of Jurisprudence
DK   *IVR* Denmark
dk.   **1.** dark **2.** deck **3.** dock
dkg   dekagram (US)
dkl   dekalitre (US)
dkm   dekametre (US)
DL   **1.** Deputy Lieutenant **2.** Doctor of Law
D/L   Demand Loan
dl   decilitre
DLit   Doctor of Literature
dlr.   dealer
DLS   Doctor of Library Science
dlvy.   delivery
dly.   daily
DM   **1.** Deutsche Mark **2.** Doctor of Medicine **3.** Doctor of Music
dm   decimetre
DMD   *Doctor Medicinae Dentalis* (*L.* Doctor of Dental Medicine)
DME   Diploma in Mechanical Engineering
DMed   Doctor of Medicine
DMet   **1.** Diploma of Meteorology **2.** Doctor of Metallurgy
DMHS   Director of Medical Health Services
DMI   Director of Military Intelligence
DMJ   Diploma of Medical Jurisprudence
DML   Doctor of Modern Languages

DMO   District Medical Officer
DMP   Diploma in Medical Psychology
DMR   Diploma in Medical Radiology
DMS   1. Director of Medical Services
2. Doctor of Medical Science
DMSO   *Chem.* dimethyl sulphoxide
DMus   Doctor of Music
DMV   Doctor of Veterinary Medicine
DMZ   demilitarized zone
DN   1. Debit Note   2. Diploma in
Nutrition
DNA   *Chem.* deoxyribonucleic acid
DNB   *Dictionary of National Biography*
DO   1. Defence Order   2. District Office
3. Doctor of Ophthalmology   4. Doctor of
Osteopathy
D/O   delivery order
do.   *ditto* (*It.* the same)
DOA   dead on arrival
d.o.b.   date of birth
doc.   document
DOD   Department of Defense (US)
DOE   Department of the Environment
DOH   Department of Health (Ireland)
dol.   1. *Mus. dolce* (*It.* sweet)   2. dollar
DOM   1. *Deo optimo maximo* (*L.* to God,
the best and greatest)   2. *IVR* Dominican
Republic
dom.   1. domain   2. domestic
3. domicile   4. dominion

Dom. Rep.   Dominican Republic

DOMS   Diploma in Ophthalmic Medicine and Surgery

DOpt   Diploma in Ophthalmics

Dor.   Doric

DORA   Defence of the Realm Act (1914)

DOS   Diploma in Orthopaedic Surgery

DOT   **1.** Department of Transportation (US) **2.** Diploma in Occupational Therapy

doz.   dozen

DP   **1.** data processing **2.** degree of polymerization **3.** Democratic Party (Aust.) **4.** diametrical pitch **5.** Diploma in Psychiatry **6.** displaced person **7.** Doctor of Philosophy

DPA   Doctor of Public Administration

DPH   **1.** Diploma in Public Health **2.** Doctor of Public Health

DPh, DPhil   Doctor of Philosophy

DPharm   Doctor of Pharmacy

DPI   Department of Public Information (of UNO)

DPM   **1.** Deputy Prime Minister **2.** Deputy Provost Marshal **3.** Diploma in Psychological Medicine

dpm   disintegrations per minute

DPP   Director of Public Prosecutions

DPS   Doctor of Public Service

dpt.   **1.** department **2.** deponent **3.** deposit **4.** depot

DPW   Department of Public Works
DR   **1.** dead reckoning **2.** deposit receipt **3.** Diploma in Radiology
Dr.   **1.** Doctor **2.** Drive
dr.   **1.** debit **2.** debtor **3.** drachma **4.** dram **5.** drawer
dram. pers.   *dramatis personae* (*L.* characters represented in the drama)
DRE   Doctor of Religious Education
drg.   drawing
DS   **1.** *Mus. dal segno* (*It.* from the sign) **2.** disseminated sclerosis **3.** Doctor of Science
DSC   **1.** Distinguished Service Cross **2.** Doctor of Surgical Chiropody
DSc   Doctor of Science
DScAgr   Doctor of Science in Agriculture
DSc(Econ)   Doctor of Science (Economics)
DScn   Doctor of Scientology
DScS   Doctor of Social Science
DSM   Distinguished Service Medal
DSO   Distinguished Service Order
d.s.p.   *decessit sine prole* (*L.* died without issue)
d.s.p.l.   *decessit sine prole legitima* (*L.* died without legitimate issue)
d.s.p.m.   *decessit sine prole mascula* (*L.* died without male issue)
d.s.p.m.s.   *decessit sine prole mascula*

superstite (*L.* died without surviving male issue)

d.s.p.s. *decessit sine prole superstite* (*L.* died without surviving issue)

d.s.p.v. *decessit sine prole virile* (*L.* died without male issue)

DSS Doctor of Social Science

DST 1. Daylight Saving Time 2. Doctor of Sacred Theology

DSW 1. Doctor of Social Welfare 2. Doctor of Social Work

DT 1. data transmission 2. delirium tremens 3. *Doctor Theologiae* (*L.* Doctor of Divinity) 4. double time

DTech Doctor of Technology

DTh, DTheol Doctor of Theology

DTI Department of Trade and Industry

DTM Diploma in Tropical Medicine

Du. 1. Duchy 2. Duke 3. Dutch

Dumb. Dumbarton

Dumf. Dumfriesshire (former county)

Dunb. Dunbartonshire (former county)

DUP Diploma of the University of Paris

dup. duplicate

Dur. Durham

DV 1. defective vision 2. *Deo volente* (*L.* God willing) 3. Douay Version (of the Bible)

DVM Doctor of Veterinary Medicine

d.v.m.   *decessit vita matris* (*L.* died in mother's lifetime)
DVMS   Doctor of Veterinary Medicine and Surgery
d.v.p.   *decessit vita patris* (*L.* died in father's lifetime)
dvr.   driver
DVS   Doctor of Veterinary Surgery
DW   Dock Warrant
dwt.   pennyweight (*denarius* + weight)
d.w.t.   dead weight tonnage
DX   *Radio* 1. distance 2. distant
DY   *IVR* Dahomey
Dy   *Chem.* dysprosium
dy.   delivery
dyn.   1. dynamics 2. dynamite 3. dynamo 4. dynamometer 5. dyne
DZ   1. *IVR* Algeria 2. Doctor of Zoology
dz.   dozen
DZool   Doctor of Zoology

E

E   1. Earl 2. Earth 3. East 4. Easter 5. Eastern 6. Eminence 7. Engineer 8. Engineering 9. England 10. English 11. *IVR* Spain 12. Excellency

e.   **1.** economics **2.** educated **3.** elder **4.** electric **5.** electromotive **6.** error **7.** excellent

EA   educational age

ea.   each

EAA   **1.** Engineer in Aeronautics and Astronautics **2.** European Athletic Association

EAAA   European Association of Advertising Agencies

EAAC   **1.** East African Airways Corporation **2.** European Agricultural Aviation Centre

EAC   Engineering Advisory Council

EADA   East African Dental Association

EADB   East African Development Bank

EAES   European Atomic Energy Society

EAHC   East African High Commission

EAIRO   East African Industrial Research Organization

EAK   *IVR* Kenya

EAM   *DP* electrical accounting machine

E & OE   errors and omissions excepted

e.a.o.n.   except as otherwise noted

EAS   estimated air speed

EAT   *IVR* Tanzania (formerly Tanganyika)

EAU   *IVR* Uganda

EAX   *DP* electronic automatic exchange

EAZ   *IVR* Tanzania (formerly Zanzibar)

EB 1. Electricity Board 2. Encyclopedia Britannica

EBC Educational Broadcasting Corporation (US)

EBCDIC *DP* extended binary coded decimal interchange code

EBU 1. European Boxing Union 2. European Broadcasting Union

EC 1. East Central 2. *IVR* Ecuador 3. Episcopal Church 4. Established Church

Ec. Ecuador

e.c. *exempli causa* (*L.* for example)

ECA 1. Economic Commission for Africa 2. Economic Cooperation Administration (now MSA) 3. European Confederation of Agriculture 4. European Congress of Accountants

ECAFE Economic Commission for Asia and the Far East

ECC *DP* error checking and correction

Eccl. Ecclesiastic(al)

Eccles. *Bib.* Ecclesiastes

Ecclus. *Bib.* Ecclesiasticus

ECE 1. Economic Commission for Europe 2. Export Council for Europe

ECG 1. electrocardiagram 2. electrocardiagraph 3. Export Credit Guarantee

ECLA Economic Commission for Latin
America
ECME Economic Commission for the
Middle East
ECNR European Council for Nuclear
Research
ecol. 1. ecological 2. ecology
econ. 1. economical 2. ecomics
3. economy
ECOSOC Economic and Social Council
(of the UN)
ECSC European Coal and Steel
Community
ECT electroconvulsive therapy
ECU English Church Union
Ecua. Ecuador
ECWA Economic Commission for
Western Asia
ED 1. Doctor of Engineering
2. Efficiency Decoration 3. Election
District (US) 4. Entertainments Duty
5. Estate Duties
ed. 1. edited 2. edition 3. editor
4. education
EDA Educational Development
Association
EdB Bachelor of Education
EDC 1. Economic Development
Committee 2. European Defence

Community **3.** *Med.* expected date of
confinement
EDD   *Med.* expected date of delivery
EdD   Doctor of Education
EDF   European Development Fund
edit.   **1.** edited **2.** edition **3.** editor
EdM   Master of Education
edn.   edition
EDP   electronic data processing
EDS   English Dialect Society
EDT   Eastern Daylight Time (US)
educ.   **1.** educated **2.** education
3. educational
EE   **1.** Early English **2.** Electrical
Engineer(ing) **3.** Employment Exchange
4. Envoy Extraordinary
e.e.   errors excepted
EE & MP   Envoy Extraordinary and
Minister Plenipotentiary
EEC   European Economic Community
EEG   **1.** electroencephalogram
2. electroencephalograph
EEOC   Equal Employment Opportunities
Commission
EETS   Early English Text Society
EF   **1.** Expeditionary Force **2.** extra fine
EETPU   Electrical, Electronic,
Telecommunications and Plumbing Union
EFL   English as a foreign language
EFT   electronic funds transfer

EFTA (ef'tə) European Free Trade Association

EFU European Football Union

Eg. 1. Egypt(ian) 2. Egyptology

e.g. *exempli gratia* (*L.* for example)

Egypt. Egyptian

EHF extremely high frequency

e.h.p. effective horse power

EHV extra high voltage

EI 1. East Indian 2. East Indies

EIB European Investment Bank

EIC Engineering Institute of Canada

EInd. East Indian

EIS Educational Institute of Scotland

EKG 1. electrocardiagram 2. electrocardiagraph

ELDO European Launcher Development Organization

elect. 1. electric 2. electrical 3. electricity

elem. 1. element 2. elementary

elev. elevation

Eliz. Elizabethan

ELT English Language Teaching

EM 1. Earl Marshal 2. Edward Medal 3. electromagnetic 4. electromotive 5. Engineer of Mines 6. enlisted man 7. Master of Engineering (US)

EMA European Monetary Agreement

EMB Egg Marketing Board

Emb. **1.** Embankment **2.** Embassy
embryol. embryology
emer. emergency
EMF, emf electromotive force
EMI Electrical and Musical Industries Ltd.
Emp. **1.** Emperor **2.** Empire
3. Empress
EMR electronic magnetic resonance
EMS **1.** Emergency Medical Service
2. European Monetary System
EMU, emu electromagnetic unit
enc. **1.** enclosed **2.** enclosure
3. encyclopedia
encl. **1.** enclosed **2.** enclosure
ency. encyclopedia
end. endorsed
ENE east-northeast
ENEA European Nuclear Energy Agency
Eng. **1.** England **2.** English
eng. **1.** engine **2.** engineer
3. engineering **4.** engraved **5.** engraver
6. engraving
EngD Doctor of Engineering
engin. engineering
Engl. **1.** England **2.** English
engr. **1.** engineer **2.** engineering
3. engraved **4.** engraver **5.** engraving
enl. **1.** enlarged **2.** enlisted
Ens. Ensign

ENSA (en'sə) Entertainments National Services Association

ENT ear, nose and throat

ent., entom. entomology

Ent. Sta. Hall Entered at Stationers' Hall

Env. Envoy

env. envelope

Env. Ext. Envoy Extraordinary

EO 1. Education Officer 2. Emergency Operation 3. Engineer Officer 4. Executive Officer

e.o. *ex officio* (*L.* by virtue of office)

EOC Equal Opportunities Commission

e.o.d. every other day

e.o.m. 1. *DP* end of message 2. end of the month 3. every other month

EONR European Organization for Nuclear Research

EP 1. electroplate 2. extended play (record)

Ep. Epistle

e.p. *Chess en passant* (*Fr.* in passing)

EPA 1. Employment Protection Act 2. Environmental Protection Agency (US) 3. European Productivity Agency

EPD Excess Profits Duty

Eph. *Bib.* Ephesians

epil. epilogue

Epiph. Epiphany

Epis. **1.** Episcopal **2.** Episcopalian **3.** Epistle
Epist. Epistle
epit. **1.** epitaph **2.** epitome
EPNS electroplated nickel silver
EPT Excess Profits Tax
EPU European Payments Union
EQ educational quotient
eq. **1.** equal **2.** equalizer **3.** equation **4.** equator **5.** equipment **6.** equitable **7.** equity **8.** equivalent
eqn. equation
Equity British Actors' Equity Association
equiv. equivalent
ER **1.** East Riding **2.** *Eduardus Rex* (*L.* King Edward) **3.** *Elizabeth Regina* (*L.* Queen Elizabeth)
Er *Chem.* erbium
ERA Emergency Relief Administration
ERDE Engineering Research and Development Establishment
ERNIE (ɐr′nē) Electronic Random Number Indicator Equipment
ERP European Recovery Programme
ERS Earnings Related Supplement
Es *Chem.* einsteinium
ESB Electricity Supply Board (Ireland)
ESCAP Economic and Social Commission for Asia and the Pacific
Esd. *Bib.* Esdras

ESE   east-southeast
Esk.   Eskimo
ESL   English as a second language
ESN   educationally subnormal
ESP   extrasensory perception
esp.   especially
Esq.   Esquire
ESR   electron spin resonance
ESRO   European Space Research Organization
EST   **1.** Eastern Standard Time (US) **2.** electro-shock treatment
Est.   **1.** Established **2.** Estate
est.   **1.** estimated **2.** estuary
estab.   established
ESTEC   European Space Technology Centre
Esth.   *Bib.* Esther
ESTI   European Space Technology Institute
ESU, esu   electrostatic unit
ET   **1.** *IVR* Egypt **2.** elapsed time **3.** Entertainments Tax
Et   *Chem.* ethyl
ETA   estimated time of arrival
et al.   **1.** *et alibi* (*L.* and elsewhere) **2.** *et alii* (*L.* and others)
etc.   *et cetera* (*L.* and so on)
ETD   estimated time of departure
Eth.   **1.** Ethiopia(n) **2.** Ethiopic

ethnol.   ethnology
ETU   Electrical Trades Union
ETUC   European Trade Union
Confederation
ETV   Educational Television
etym.   1. etymological 2. etymology
EU   Evangelical Union
Eu   *Chem.* europium
Eu., Eur.   1. Europe 2. European
Euratom   European Atomic Energy
Community
EV, e.v.   electron volt
EVA   *Astron.* extravehicular activity
evg.   evening
evid.   evidence
evol.   evolution
e.w.   each way
EWR   early warning radar
Ex.   1. Exeter 2. *Bib.* Exodus
ex.   1. examination 2. examined
3. example 4. excellent 5. except
6. exception 7. exchange 8. excluding
9. excursion 10. executed 11. executive
12. exempt 13. express 14. export
15. extra 16. extract
exam.   1. examination 2. examined
3. examinee 4. examiner
Exc.   Excellency
exc.   1. excellent 2. except
3. exception 4. excursion

exch. 1. exchange 2. exchequer
excl. 1. exclamation 2. excluding
3. exclusive
ex d., ex div. *Fin.* ex dividend
exec. 1. executive 2. executor
execx. executrix
exh. exhibition
ex int. *Fin.* excluding interest
ex lib. *ex libris* (*L.* from the library of)
Exod. *Bib.* Exodus
ex off. *ex officio* (*L.* by virtue of office)
exp. 1. expanded 2. expedition
3. expenses 4. experienced
5. experiment 6. expiration 7. expired
8. exponential 9. export 10. exporter
11. express
expl. 1. explained 2. explanatory
3. explosion 4. explosive
expn. exposition
exptl. experimental
exr. executor
exrx. executrix
ext. 1. extension 2. exterior
3. external 4. extinct 5. extra
6. extract 7. extreme
extn. extension
Ez. *Bib.* Ezra
Ezek. *Bib.* Ezekiel

F

F **1.** Fahrenheit **2.** farad **3.** Father
4. fathom **5.** February **6.** Fellow
7. Finance **8.** *Chem.* fluorine **9.** folio
10. *Mus.* forte (*It.* loud) **11.** *IVR* France
12. French **13.** frequency **14.** Friday
15. function
f. **1.** farad **2.** farthing **3.** fathom
4. feet **5.** female **6.** feminine **7.** filly
8. fine **9.** fluid **10.** folio **11.** following
12. foot **13.** *forte* **14.** foul **15.** franc
16. frequency **17.** from **18.** furlong
FA **1.** Faculty of Actuaries **2.** Fanny
Adams **3.** Field Artillery **4.** Football
Association
f.a. **1.** free alongside **2.** freight agent
FAA **1.** Federal Aviation Agency (US)
2. Fellow of the Australian Academy of
Science **3.** Film Artists' Association
4. Fleet Air Arm
FAAAS **1.** Fellow of the American
Academy of Arts and Sciences **2.** Fellow of
the American Association for the
Advancement of Science
Fac. Faculty
fac. **1.** facsimile **2.** factor **3.** factory

FACC Fellow of the Australian College of Cardiology

FACCA Fellow of the Association of Certified and Corporate Accountants

FACE Fellow of the Australian College of Education

FACP Fellow of the American College of Physicians

FACS Fellow of the American College of Surgeons

Fah. Fahrenheit

FAI Football Association of Ireland

FAIA **1.** Fellow of the American Institute of Architects **2.** Fellow of the Association of International Accountants

FAIAS Fellow of the Australian Institute of Agricultural Science

FAIB Fellow of the Australian Institute of Builders

FAIC Fellow of the American Institute of Chemists

FAII Fellow of the Australian Insurance Institute

FAIM Fellow of the Australian Institute of Management

FAIMS Fellow of the Indian Academy of Medical Sciences

FAM Free and Accepted Masons

fam. **1.** familiar **2.** family

FAMA Fellow of the American Medical Association

FANY First Aid Nursing Yeomanry

FAO Food and Agriculture Organization

FAQ fair average quality

FAR Federation of Arab Republics

FAS 1. Faculty of Architects and Surveyors 2. Federation of American Scientists 3. Fellow of the Antiquarian Society 4. Fellow of the Society of Arts 5. Foreign Agricultural Service (US)

f.a.s. free alongside ship

FASE Fellow of the Antiquarian Society, Edinburgh

fath. fathom

FBA 1. Federal Bar Association (US) 2. Fellow of the British Academy

FBAA Fellow of the British Association of Accountants and Auditors

FBHI Fellow of the British Horological Institute

FBI Federal Bureau of Investigation (US)

FBIA Fellow of the Bankers' Institute of Australasia

FBIM Fellow of the British Institute of Management

FBOA Fellow of the British Optical Association

FBPsS Fellow of the British Psychological Society

FBritIRE Fellow of the British Institution of Radio Engineers (now **FIERE**)

FBS Fellow of the Botanical Society

FBU Fire Brigades Union

FC **1.** Football Club **2.** Free Church

f.c. **1.** fire control **2.** *Ptg.* follow copy **3.** foot candle

FCA **1.** Farm Credit Administration (US) **2.** Fellow of the Institute of Chartered Accountants in England and Wales

FCAA Fellow of the Australasian Insitute of Cost Accountants

FCA(Aust) Fellow of the Institute of Chartered Accountants in Australia

fcap. foolscap

FCBA Fellow of the Canadian Bankers' Association

FCBCC Federation of Commonwealth and British Chambers of Commerce

FCC Federal Communications Commission (US)

FCCC Federation of Commonwealth Chambers of Commerce

FCCS Fellow of the Corporation of Certified Secretaries

FCGI Fellow of the City and Guilds of London Institute

FCI Fellow of the Institute of Commerce

FCIA Fellow of the Corporation of Insurance Agents

FCIB Fellow of the Corporation of Insurance Brokers

FCIC Fellow of the Chemical Institute of Canada

FCII Fellow of the Chartered Insurance Institute

FCIPA Fellow of the Chartered Institute of Patent Agents

FCIS Fellow of the Chartered Institute of Secretaries

FCMA Fellow of the Institute of Cost and Management Accountants

FCO Foreign and Commonwealth Office

FCP Fellow of the College of Preceptors

FCS 1. Fellow of the Chemical Society 2. Fellow of the Corporation of Secretaries

FCT Federal Capital Territory

FCWA Fellow of the Institute of Cost and Works Accountants (now **FCMA**)

FD 1. *Fidei Defensor* (*L.* Defender of the Faith) 2. Fire Department 3. free dock

fd. 1. forward 2. found 3. founded

FDA Food and Drug Administration (US)

FDC 1. first-day cover 2. *fleur de coin* (*Fr.* mint condition)

FDIC Federal Deposit Insurance Corporation (US)

FDS Fellow in Dental Surgery

Fe *Chem.* iron
Feb. February
fec. *fecit* (*L.* he/she made)
FECB Foreign Exchange Control Board
fed. **1.** federal **2.** federated
3. federation
FEIS Fellow of the Educational Institute of Scotland
fem. **1.** female **2.** feminine
FEP Fair Employment Practice
FEPC Fair Employment Practices Committee (US)
FET **1.** Federal Excise Tax **2.** field-effect transistor
ff *Mus. fortissimo* (*It.* very loud)
ff. **1.** folios **2.** the following
FFA **1.** Fellow of the Faculty of Actuaries (Scotland) **2.** Future Farmers of America
f.f.a. free from alongside
FFAS Fellow of the Faculty of Architects and Surveyors
FFC **1.** Foreign Funds Control **2.** free from chlorine
FFI free from infection
FFPS Fellow of the Royal Faculty of Physicians and Surgeons
FFR Fellow of the Faculty of Radiologists
FFV First Families of Virginia
FGS Fellow of the Geological Society

FGSM Fellow of the Guildhall School of Music

FH 1. Field Hospital 2. fire hydrant

FHA 1. Federal Housing Administration (US) 2. Fellow of the Institute of Hospital Administrators 3. Finance Houses Association

FHCI Fellow of the Hotel and Catering Institute

FHR Federal House of Representatives

FI Falkland Islands

FIA Fellow of the Institute of Actuaries

FIAC Fellow of the Institute of Company Accountants

FIAII Fellow of the Incorporated Australian Insurance Institute

FIAL Fellow of the International Institute of Arts and Letters

FIANZ Fellow of the Institute of Actuaries of New Zealand

FIArb Fellow of the Institute of Arbitrators

FIAS Fellow of the Institute of the Aerospace Sciences (US)

FIAT (fē'ət) *Fabbrica Italiana Automobile Turino*

FIB 1. Fellow of the Institute of Bankers 2. Fellow of the Institute of Building

FIBA Fellow of the Institute of Banking Associations

FIBP Fellow of the Institute of British Photographers

FICA Federal Insurance Contributions Act (US)

FICE Fellow of the Institution of Civil Engineers

FICI Fellow of the Institute of Chemistry of Ireland

FICS Fellow of the Institute of Chartered Shipbrokers

fict. 1. fiction 2. fictitious

FID Fellow of the Institute of Directors

Fid. Def. *Fidei Defensor* (*L.* Defender of the Faith)

FIDO 1. Film Industry Defence Organization 2. (fī'dō) Fog Investigation and Dispersal Operation

FIEE Fellow of the Institution of Electrical Engineers

FIEEE Fellow of the Institution of Electrical and Electronics Engineers

FIERE Fellow of the Institute of Electronic and Radio Engineers

FIFA (fē'fə) *Fédération Internationale de Football Association* (*Fr.* International Association Football Federation)

FIFE Fellow of the Institution of Fire Engineers

fig. 1. figuratively 2. figure

FIH Fellow of the Institute of Hygiene

FIHVE Fellow of the Institution of Heating and Ventilating Engineers

FII 1. Federation of Irish Industries 2. Fellow of the Imperial Institute

FIITech Fellow of the Institute of Industrial Technicians

FIL Fellow of the Institute of Linguists

FIM Fellow of the Institution of Metallurgists

FIMechE Fellow of the Institution of Mechanical Engineers

FIMI Fellow of the Institute of the Motor Industry

FIN Fellow of the Institute of Navigation

Fin. 1. Finland 2. Finnish

fin. 1. final 2. finance 3. financial 4. finish

Finn. Finnish

FInstArb Fellow of the Institute of Arbitrators

FInstCh Fellow of the Institute of Chiropodists

FInstD Fellow of the Institute of Directors

FInstF Fellow of the Institute of Fuel

FInstHE Fellow of the Institution of Highway Engineers

FInstMet Fellow of the Institute of Metals

FInstP Fellow of the Institute of Physics

FInstPet Fellow of the Institute of Petroleum

FInstT   Fellow of the Institute of
Transport
FIO   Fellow of the Institute of
Ophthalmology
FIOB   Fellow of the Insitute of Building
FIPHE   Fellow of the Institution of Public
Health Engineers
FIPlantE   Fellow of the Institution of Plant
Engineers
FIPM   Fellow of the Institute of Personnel
Management
FIPtgM   Fellow of the Institute of Printing
Management
FIQS   Fellow of the Institute of Quantity
Surveyors
FIRE   Fellow of the Institute of Radio
Engineers (US)
FIWE   Fellow of the Institute of Water
Engineers
FJI   1. Fellow of the Institute of
Journalists 2. *IVR* Fiji
FL   1. Flight Lieutenant 2. *IVR*
Liechtenstein
Fl.   1. Flanders 2. Flemish
fl.   1. floor 2. florin 3. *floruit* (*L.*
flourished) 4. fluid
FLA   Fellow of the Library Association
Fla.   Florida
FLB   Federal Land Bank (US)

FLCM   Fellow of the London College of
Music
fld.   field
fl. dr.   fluid dram
Flem.   Flemish
Flor.   Florida
flor.   *floruit* (*L.* flourished)
fl. oz.   fluid ounce
FLS   Fellow of the Linnean Society
flt.   flight
FM   1. Field Marshal 2. frequency
modulation
Fm   *Chem.* fermium
fm.   1. fathom 2. from
FMB   1. Federal Maritime Board (US)
2. Federation of Master Builders
FMC   Federal Maritime Commission (US)
FMCS   Federal Mediation and Conciliation
Service (US)
FMD   foot and mouth disease
FMF   Food Manufacturers' Federation
FMN   flavin mononucleotide
fn.   footnote
FNMA   Federal National Mortgage
Association (US)
FNZIA   Fellow of the New Zealand
Institute of Architects
FNZIC   Fellow of the New Zealand
Institute of Chemistry

FNZIM Fellow of the New Zealand Institute of Management

FNZLA Fellow of the New Zealand Library Association

FNZSA Fellow of the New Zealand Society of Accountants

FO 1. Field Officer 2. Flying Officer 3. Foreign Office (now **FCO**)

fo. folio

f.o.b. free on board

FOBS fractional orbital bombardment system

FOC 1. Father of the Chapel (printing unions) 2. free of charge

FOE Friends of Europe

fol. 1. folio 2. followed 3. following

foll. following

for. 1. foreign 2. forestry

f.o.r. free on rail

fort. 1. fortification 2. fortified

FORTRAN (fôr'tran) *DP Formula Translation*

FOSDIC (foz'dik) Film Optical Sensing Device for Input to Computer

FP 1. fireplug (US) 2. fire policy 3. floating policy 4. former pupil 5. Free Presbyterian 6. freezing point 7. fully paid

fp *Mus. forte piano* (*It.* loud and then immediately soft)

f.p. 1. foot-pound 2. freezing point

FPA 1. Family Planning Association
2. Fire Protection Association 3. Foreign
Press Association

FPC 1. Federal Power Commission (US)
2. fish protein concentrate

f.p.m. feet per minute

FPO 1. Field Post Office 2. Fire
Prevention Officer 3. Fleet Post Office
(US)

FPS 1. Fellow of the Pharmaceutical
Society 2. Fellow of the Philological
Society 3. Fellow of the Physical Society

f.p.s. 1. feet per second 2. foot-pound-
second 3. *Phot.* frames per second

Fr *Chem.* francium

Fr. 1. Father 2. France 3. *frater* (*L.*
brother) 4. *Frau* 5. French 6. Friar
7. Friday

fr. 1. fragment 2. franc 3. frequent
4. from

f.r. *folio recto* (*L.* right hand page)

FRACI Fellow of the Royal Australian
Chemical Institute

FRACP Fellow of the Royal Australasian
College of Physicians

FRACS Fellow of the Royal Australasian
College of Surgeons

FRAeS Fellow of the Royal Aeronautical
Society

FRAI Fellow of the Royal Anthropological Institute

FRAIA Fellow of the Royal Australian Institute of Architects

FRAIC Fellow of the Royal Architectural Institute of Canada

FRAM Fellow of the Royal Academy of Music

Frank. Frankish

FRAS Fellow of the Royal Astronomical Society

FRB 1. Federal Reserve Bank 2. Federal Reserve Board

FRBS Fellow of the Royal Society of British Sculptors

FRCA Fellow of the Royal College of Art

FRCM Fellow of the Royal College of Music

FRCO Fellow of the Royal College of Organists

FRCOG Fellow of the Royal College of Obstetricians and Gynaecologists

FRCP Fellow of the Royal College of Physicians

FRCS Fellow of the Royal College of Surgeons

FRCVS Fellow of the Royal College of Veterinary Surgeons

FREconS Fellow of the Royal Economic Society

freq. 1. frequent **2.** frequentative **3.** frequently

FRES Fellow of the Royal Entomological Society

FRFPS Fellow of the Royal Faculty of Physicians and Surgeons

FRGS Fellow of the Royal Geographical Society

FRHistS Fellow of the Royal Historical Society

FRHortS Fellow of the Royal Horticultural Society

Fri. Friday

FRIA Fellow of the Royal Irish Academy

FRIAS Fellow of the Royal Incorporation of Architects in Scotland

FRIBA Fellow of the Royal Institute of British Architects

FRIC Fellow of the Royal Institute of Chemistry

FRICS Fellow of the Royal Institute of Chartered Surveyors

FRIIA Fellow of the Royal Institute of International Affairs

FRINA Fellow of the Royal Institution of Naval Architects

FRIPA Fellow of the Royal Institute of Public Administration

FRIPHH Fellow of the Royal Institute of Public Health and Hygiene

Fris. Frisian

Frl. *Fräulein*

FRMetSoc Fellow of the Royal Meteorological Society

front. frontispiece

FRPS Fellow of the Royal Photographic Society

FRS **1.** Federal Reserve System **2.** Fellow of the Royal Society

Frs. Frisian

FRSA Fellow of the Royal Society of Arts

FRSAMD Fellow of the Royal Scottish Academy of Music and Drama

FRSC Fellow of the Royal Society of Canada

FRSE Fellow of the Royal Society of Edinburgh

FRSL Fellow of the Royal Society of Literature

FRSM Fellow of the Royal Society of Medicine

FRSNZ Fellow of the Royal Society of New Zealand

FRSS Fellow of the Royal Statistical Society

FRSSA Fellow of the Royal Scottish Society of Arts

frt. freight

FRZS Fellow of the Royal Zoological Society

f.s. foot-second
FSA Fellow of the Society of Antiquaries
FSAA Fellow of the Society of
Incorporated Accountants and Auditors
FSC 1. Federal Supreme Court (US)
2. Fellow of the Society of Chiropodists
FSE Fellow of the Society of Engineers
FSF Fellow of the Institute of Shipping
and Forwarding Agents
FSG Fellow of the Society of Genealogists
FSH follicle-stimulating hormone
FSLIC Federal Savings and Loan
Insurance Corporation (US)
FSS Fellow of the Statistical Society
FSSU Federated Superannuation Scheme
for Universities
FSVA Fellow of the Incorporated Society
of Valuers and Auctioneers
ft. 1. feet 2. foot 3. fort 4. fortification
FTC Federal Trade Commission (US)
fth. fathom
FTI Fellow of the Textile Institute
ft-lb foot-pound
FTS Federal Telecommunications System
(US)
FUE Federated Union of Employers
fur. furlong
fut. future
f.v. *folio verso* (*L.* left-hand page)
fwd. forward

f.w.d. **1.** four-wheel drive **2.** front-wheel drive
FY Fiscal Year
FYI for your information
fz *forzando* (*It.* to be strongly accentuated)
FZS Fellow of the Zoological Society

G

G **1.** *Phys.* conductance **2.** gauge **3.** German **4.** giga **5.** grain **6.** gram **7.** grand **8.** *Phys.* gravitational constant **9.** guilder **10.** guinea **11.** gulf **12.** gravity
g **1.** gram(me) **2.** *Phys.* gravitational acceleration
g. **1.** *Psychol.* general intelligence **2.** genitive **3.** goalkeeper **4.** guinea
GA **1.** General Agent **2.** General Assembly **3.** Geographical Association
Ga *Chem.* gallium
Ga. **1.** Gallic **2.** Georgia
g.a. general average
Gael. Gaelic
Gal. *Bib.* Galatians
gal., gall. gallon

galv.   **1.** galvanic **2.** galvanism

gam.   gamut

GAO   General Accounting Office

GAR   Grand Army of the Republic (US)

GATT (gat)   General Agreement on Tariffs and Trade

GAW   guaranteed annual wage

gaz.   **1.** gazette **2.** gazetteer

GB   *IVR* Great Britain and Northern Ireland

GBA   *IVR* Alderney

GBE   Grand Cross of the Order of the British Empire

GBG   *IVR* Guernsey

g.b.h.   grievous bodily harm

GBJ   *IVR* Jersey

GBM   *IVR* Isle of Man

GBZ   *IVR* Gibraltar

GC   **1.** George Cross **2.** Golf Club

GCA   **1.** ground controlled approach **2.** *IVR* Guatemala

g-cal.   gram calorie

GCB   Grand Cross of the Order of the Bath

GCD   greatest common divisor

GCE   General Certificate of Education

GCF   greatest common factor

GCH   Grand Cross of Hanover

GCIE   Knight Grand Commander of the Order of the Indian Empire

GCLH Grand Cross of the Legion of Honour

GCM General Court Martial

GCMG Knight *or* Dame Grand Cross of the Order of St Michael and St George

GCR ground controlled radar

gcs gigacycles per second

GCSI Knight Grand Commander of the Order of the Star of India

GCT Greenwich Civil Time

GCVO Grand Cross of the Royal Victorian Order

GD 1. Grand Duchess 2. Grand Duke

Gd *Chem.* gadolinium

gd. 1. good 2. guard

GDBA Guide Dogs for the Blind Association

gde. gourde

Gdns. Gardens

GDR German Democratic Republic

gds. goods

Ge *Chem.* germanium

GEC General Electric Company Ltd.

GED general educational development

Gen. 1. General 2. *Bib.* Genesis 3. Geneva

gen. 1. gender 2. general 3. generally 4. generator 5. generic 6. genetics 7. genitive 8. genuine 9. genus

geneal. genealogy

genit. genitive
genl. general
gent gentleman
Geo. Georgia
geod. 1. geodesy 2. geodetic
geog. 1. geographer 2. geographic
3. geographical 4. geography
geol. 1. geologic 2. geological
3. geologist 4. geology
geom. 1. geometric 2. geometrical
3. geometrician 4. geometry
Ger. German(y)
ger. gerund(ive)
GeV giga-electronvolts
GFR German Federal Republic
GFS Girls' Friendly Society
GFTU General Federation of Trade Unions
GG 1. Girl Guides 2. Governor General
3. Grenadier Guards
g.gr. great gross, ie 144 dozen
GH *IVR* Ghana
GHI Good Housekeeping Institute
GHQ General Headquarters
gHz gigahertz
GI 1. gastrointestinal 2. general issue
3. Government Issue
gi. gill
Gib. Gibraltar
GJ gigajoule

Gk. Greek
gl. 1. glass 2. gloss
g/l grams per litre
Glam. Glamorganshire (former county)
Glas. Glasgow
GLB Girls' Life Brigade
GLC Greater London Council
gld. guilder
GLORIA (glôr′ē ə) Geological Long Range Asdic
Glos. Gloucestershire
gloss. glossary
glt. gilt
GM 1. Geiger-Müller counter 2. General Manager 3. George Medal 4. Grand Master 5. Guided Missile
gm gram
gm² grammes per square metre
GMB Grand Master of the Order of the Bath
GMBE Grand Master of the Order of the British Empire
GMC General Medical Council
Gmc. Germanic
GMIE Grand Master of the Order of the Indian Empire
GMKP Grand Master of the Knights of St Patrick
GMMG Grand Master of the Order of St Michael and St George

GMP   Grand Master of the Order of St Patrick

g.m.q.   good merchantable quality

GMSI   Grand Master of the Order of the Star of India

GMT   Greenwich Mean Time

GMWU   National Union of General and Municipal Workers

GNC   General Nursing Council

GNP   Gross National Product

Gnr.   Gunner

gns.   guineas

GO   General Order

GOC   General Officer Commanding

GOM   Grand Old Man

GOP   Grand Old Party, ie Republican Party (US)

Goth.   Gothic

Gov.   1. Government 2. Governor

Govt.   Government

GP   1. Gallup Poll 2. *Med.* general paresis 3. *Mus.* general pause 4. General Practitioner 5. general purpose 6. *Gloria Patri* (*L.* Glory to the Father) 7. Graduated Pension 8. Grand Prix

gp.   group

g.p.   *Ptg.* great primer

GPA   grade-point average (US)

Gp. Capt.   Group Captain

GPI   general paralysis of the insane

gpm gallons per minute
GPO 1. General Post Office
  2. Government Printing Office (US)
gps gallons per second
GPU General Postal Union
GR 1. *Georgius Rex* (*L.* King George)
  2. *IVR* Greece
Gr. 1. Grecian 2. Greece 3. Greek
gr. 1. grade 2. grain 3. grammar
  4. gravity 5. great 6. gross 7. group
  8. gunner
grad. 1. gradient 2. graduate
gram. 1. grammar 2. grammarian
  3. grammatical
Gr. Br. Great Britain
GRC glass reinforced cement
gro. gross
gr. wt. gross weight
GS 1. General Secretary 2. General
Service 3. General Staff 4. Geological
Society 5. Girl Scouts (US) 6. ground
speed
gs. guineas
GSA 1. General Services Administration
  2. Girl Scouts of America
GSC General Staff Corps
gsm grammes per square metre (gm^2 is
preferred)
GSO General Staff Officer
GSP good service pension

GT **1.** Grand Tourer **2.** gross ton
gt. **1.** gilt **2.** great **3.** *gutta* (*L.* a drop)
GTC **1.** General Teaching Council
(Scotland) **2.** good till cancelled *or*
countermanded **3.** Government Training
Centre
gtd. guaranteed
GTS **1.** gas turbine ship **2.** Greenwich
Time Signal
GU **1.** gastric ulcer **2.** genitourinary
guar. guaranteed
Guat. Guatemala
Guin. Guinea
GUY *IVR* Guyana
g.v. gravimetric volume
GW gigawatt
gym. **1.** gymnasium **2.** gymnastics
gyn. **1.** gynaecological **2.** gynaecology

H

H **1.** hard (pencils) **2.** hecto- **3.** *Phys.*
henry **4.** heroin **5.** hospital **6.** *IVR*
Hungary **7.** hydrant **8.** *Chem.* hydrogen
9. *Phys.* planck constant
h. **1.** harbour **2.** hard **3.** height
4. high **5.** hit **6.** horizontal **7.** *Mus.*

horn **8.** hour (also **h**) **9.** hundred
10. husband

ha   hectare

h.a.   **1.** heir apparent **2.** *hoc anno* (*L.* in this year)

Hab.   *Bib.* Habakkuk

hab.   habitat

HAC   Honourable Artillery Company

Hag.   *Bib.* Haggai

h & c   hot and cold (water)

Hants.   Hampshire

HAS   Highland and Agricultural Society

Haw.   Hawaii(an)

HB   hard black (pencils)

Hb   haemoglobin

hbar   hectobar

HBM   His *or* Her Britannic Majesty

HC   **1.** Heralds' College **2.** Holy Communion **3.** House of Commons

h.c.   *honoris causa* (*L.* for the sake of honour)

HCF   **1.** highest common factor **2.** Honorary Chaplain to the Forces

HCI   Hotel and Catering Institute

HCJ   High Court Judge

HCM   His *or* Her Catholic Majesty

hcp.   handicap

HD   heavy duty

hd.   **1.** hand **2.** head

hdbk.   handbook

hdqrs. headquarters
hdw. hardware
HE 1. high explosive 2. His Eminence 3. His *or* Her Excellency 4. horizontal equivalent
He *Chem.* helium
Heb. 1. Hebrew 2. *Bib.* Hebrews
hectog hectogram
hectol hectolitre
hectom hectometre
HEH His *or* Her Exalted Highness
HEIC Honourable East India Company
her. 1. heraldic 2. heraldry
herp. herpetology
Herts. Hertfordshire
HEW Department of Health, Education and Welfare (US)
hex. hexagon(al)
HF 1. high frequency 2. Holy Father
Hf *Chem.* hafnium
hf. half
HG 1. High German 2. His *or* Her Grace 3. Home Guard 4. Horse Guards
Hg *Chem.* mercury
hg hectogram
hgt. height
HGV heavy goods vehicle
HH 1. double hard (pencils) 2. His *or* Her Highness 3. His Holiness 4. His Honour

hhd.   hogshead
HHFA   Housing and Home Finance
  Agency (US)
HI   Hawaiian Islands
HIDB   Highlands and Islands Development
  Board
HIH   His *or* Her Imperial Highness
HIM   His *or* Her Imperial Majesty
Hind.   **1.** Hindi **2.** Hindu
  3. Hindustan(i)
hist.   **1.** histology **2.** historian
  3. historical **4.** history
HJ   *hic jacet* (*L.* here lies)
HJS   *hic jacet sepultus* (*L.* here lies buried)
HK   **1.** *IVR* Hong Kong **2.** House of Keys
  (Manx Parliament)
HKJ   *IVR* Jordan
HL   **1.** Honours List **2.** House of Lords
hl   hectolitre
HLD   Doctor of Humane Letters
HLI   Highland Light Infantry
HM   **1.** headmaster **2.** headmistress
  3. His *or* Her Majesty
hm   hectometre
HMAS   His *or* Her Majesty's Australian
  Ship
HMC   His *or* Her Majesty's Customs
HMCS   His *or* Her Majesty's Canadian
  Ship

HMDS His *or* Her Majesty's Diplomatic Service

HMG 1. Higher Middle German 2. His *or* Her Majesty's Government

HMI His *or* Her Majesty's Inspector

HMNZS His *or* Her Majesty's New Zealand Ship

HMP *hoc monumentum posuit* (*L.* he/she erected this monument)

HMS 1. His *or* Her Majesty's Service 2. His *or* Her Majesty's Ship

HMSO His *or* Her Majesty's Stationery Office

HMV His Master's Voice

HNC Higher National Certificate

HND Higher National Diploma

HO 1. Head Office 2. Home Office

Ho *Chem.* holmium

ho. house

Hon. 1. Honorary 2. Honourable

Hond. Honduras

Hons. Honours

Hon. Sec. Honorary Secretary

hor. 1. horizon 2. horizontal 3. horology

horol. horology

hort. 1. horticultural 2. horticulture

Hos. *Bib.* Hosea

hosp. hospital

HP 1. half pay 2. high pressure 3. High

Priest **4.** high-powered **5.** hire purchase
6. horse power **7.** Houses of Parliament
HQ Headquarters
HR **1.** Home Rule **2.** House of
Representatives (US)
hr. hour
h.r. *Baseball* home run
HRC Holy Roman Church
HRE **1.** Holy Roman Emperor **2.** Holy
Roman Empire
HRH His *or* Her Royal Highness
HRIP *hic requiescit in pace* (*L.* here rests
in peace)
HS **1.** *hic sepultus* (*L.* here is buried)
2. High School **3.** Home Secretary
h.s. *hoc sensu* (*L.* in this sense)
HSE **1.** Health and Safety Executive
2. *hic sepultus est* (*L.* here lies buried)
HSH His *or* Her Serene Highness
HSM His *or* Her Serene Majesty
HSS *Historiae Societatis Socius* (*L.*
Fellow of the Historical Society)
HT high tension
ht. **1.** heat **2.** height
Hts. Heights
HUAC (hyōō'ak) House Un-American
Activities Committee
HUD (hud) Department of Housing and
Urban Development (US)
Hung. **1.** Hungarian **2.** Hungary

Hunts.   Huntingdonshire (former county)
HV   1. high velocity   2. high voltage
HVA   Health Visitors' Association
HW   high water
h.w.   hit wicket
HWM   high water mark
hwy.   highway
hyd.   1. hydraudics   2. hydrostatics
hyp.   1. hypotenuse   2. hypothesis
   3. hypothetical
hypoth.   1. hypothesis   2. hypothetical
Hz   hertz

I

I   1. *Phys.* current   2. incisor
   3. Independence   4. *Phys.* inertia
   5. Institute   6. Institution   7. Interest
   8. International   9. intransitive
   10. *Chem.* iodine   11. Island   12. Isle
   13. *Phys.* isospin   14. *IVR* Italy
   15. *Roman Numeral for* 1
i   *Math* $\sqrt{-1}$
IA   1. Incorporated Accountant
   2. Institute of Actuaries
Ia.   Iowa
i.a.   *in absentia* (*L.* in absence)

IAA **1.** International Academy of Astronautics **2.** International Advertising Association

IAAA Irish Association of Advertising Agencies

IAAB Inter-American Association of Broadcasters

IAAF International Amateur Athletic Federation

IAAS Incorporated Association of Architects and Surveyors

IAB Industrial Advisory Board

IABA International Amateur Boxing Association

IACL **1.** International Association of Comparative Law **2.** International Association of Criminal Law

IADB **1.** Inter-American Defense Board **2.** Inter-American Development Bank

IAE Institute of Automobile Engineers

IAEA International Atomic Energy Agency

IAES Institute of Aeronautical Sciences

IAM **1.** Institute of Administrative Management **2.** Institute of Advanced Motorists **3.** International Association of Machinists

IArb Institute of Arbitrators

IAS **1.** indicated air speed **2.** Institute for Advanced Studies **3.** Institute of

Aeronautical Sciences (US) **4.** Institute of
Aerospace Sciences (US) **5.** Institute of
Applied Science, Chicago
IATA International Air Transport
Association
IB **1.** Institute of Bankers **2.** Institute of
Building
ib. *ibidem* (*L.* in the same place)
IBA **1.** Independent Broadcasting
Authority **2.** Institute of British
Architects **3.** International Bankers'
Association **4.** International Bar
Association
IBB Institute of British Bankers
IBC International Broadcasting
Corporation
IBE Institute of British Engineers
ibid. *ibidem* (*L.* in the same place)
IBiol Institute of Biology
IBK Institute of Bookkeepers
IBM International Business Machines
Corporation
IBP Institute of British Photographers
IBRD International Bank for
Reconstruction and Development
IBS Institute of Bankers in Scotland
IBWM International Bureau of Weights
and Measures
IC integrated circuit
i/c **1.** in charge **2.** internal combustion

ICA **1.** Industrial Catering Association **2.** Institute of Chartered Accountants of England and Wales **3.** Institute of Company Accountants **4.** Institute of Contemporary Art **5.** International Communication Association **6.** International Cooperative Alliance

ICAO International Civil Aviation Organization

ICAS **1.** Institute of Chartered Accountants of Scotland **2.** International Council of Aeronautical Sciences

ICBM intercontinental ballistic missile

ICC **1.** International Chamber of Commerce **2.** International Control Commission **3.** Interstate Commerce Commission (US)

ICD Institute of Civil Defence

ICDO International Civil Defence Organization

ICE **1.** Institute of Chemical Engineers **2.** Institution of Civil Engineers **3.** internal combustion engine

Ice. **1.** Iceland **2.** Icelandic

ICEI Institution of Civil Engineers of Ireland

Icel. **1.** Iceland **2.** Icelandic

ICEM Intergovernmental Committee for European Migration

ICFTU International Confederation of Free Trade Unions

IChemE Institution of Chemical Engineers

ichth. ichthyology

ICI 1. Imperial Chemical Industries 2. Institute of Chemistry of Ireland

ICJ International Court of Justice

ICMA Institute of Cost and Management Accountants

ICOM International Council of Museums

icon. 1. iconographic 2. iconography

ICS 1. Institute of Chartered Shipbrokers 2. International Chamber of Shipping 3. International College of Surgeons (US)

ICSH interstitial cell-stimulating hormone

ICSID International Centre for Settlement of Investment Disputes

ICST Imperial College of Science and Technology

ICTU Irish Congress of Trade Unions

ICU intensive care unit

ICWA Institute of Cost and Works Accountants (now **ICMA**)

ID 1. identification 2. inside diameter 3. Institute of Directors 4. Intelligence Department

Id. Idaho

id. *idem* (*L.* the same)

IDA 1. Industrial Development

Authority **2.** International Development Association **3.** Irish Dental Association
Ida.   Idaho
IDB   **1.** illicit diamond buying **2.** Inter-American Development Bank
IDDD   international direct distance dialing (US)
IDN   *in Dei nomine* (*L.* in God's name)
IDP   **1.** integrated data processing **2.** international driving permit
IDS   **1.** Institute of Dental Surgery **2.** Institute of Development Studies
IE   Indo-European
i.e.   *id est* (*L.* that is)
IEA   **1.** Institute of Economic Affairs **2.** International Economic Association
IEC   International Electrotechnical Commission
IED   Institution of Engineering Designers
IEE   Institution of Electrical Engineers
IERE   Institution of Electronic and Radio Engineers
IF   intermediate frequency
IFA   **1.** Incorporated Faculty of Arts **2.** Irish Football Association
IFAW   International Fund for Animal Welfare
IFC   International Finance Corporation
IFE   Institution of Fire Engineers
IFR   instrument flight rules

IFS   Irish Free State
IFT   International Federation of Translators
IG   1. Indo-Germanic 2. Inspector General
IGasE   Institution of Gas Engineers
ign.   1. ignites 2. ignition 3. *ignotus* (*L.* unknown)
IGY   International Geophysical Year
IHA   1. Institute of Hospital Administrators 2. International Hotel Association
IHE   Institution of Highway Engineers
IHP   indicated horse power
IHVE   Institution of Heating and Ventilating Engineers
IIAL   International Institute of Arts and Letters
IIAS   International Institute of Administrative Sciences
IIS   Irish Institute of Secretaries
IL   1. Institute of Linguists 2. *IVR* Israel
ILA   1. Institute of Landscape Architects 2. International Law Association
ILC   International Law Commission
ILE   Institution of Locomotive Engineers
ILEA   Inner London Education Authority
Ill.   Illinois
ill., illus.   1. illustrated 2. illustration
ILO   International Labour Organization

imp.

ILP Independent Labour Party
ILS 1. Incorporated Law Society
2. instrument landing system
ILTF International Lawn Tennis
Federation
IM 1. Institute of Music 2. Institution of
Metallurgists 3. intramuscular 4. Isle of
Man
IMA Irish Medical Association
IMarE Institute of Marine Engineers
IMC Institute of Management Consultants
IMCO Intergovernmental Maritime
Consultative Organization (US)
IME 1. Institution of Mechanical
Engineers 2. Institution of Mining
Engineers 3. Institution of Municipal
Engineers
IMechE Institution of Mechanical
Engineers
IMF International Monetary Fund
IMI 1. Institute of the Motor Industry
2. Irish Management Institute
IMinE Institution of Mining Engineers
imit. 1. imitation 2. imitative
IMM Institute of Mining and Metallurgy
Imp. 1. *Imperator* (L. Emperor)
2. *Imperatrix* (L. Empress) 3. Imperial
imp. 1. imperative 2. imperfect
3. imperial 4. impersonal 5. implement
6. import 7. important 8. importer

9. *imprimatur* (*L.* let it be printed)
10. imprint 11. improper 12. improved
13. improvement
imper. imperative
imperf. 1. imperfect 2. imperforate
impers. impersonal
impf. imperfect
imp. gall. imperial gallon
impv. imperative
IMTA Institute of Municipal Treasurers and Accountants
IMunE Institution of Municipal Engineers
IMVS Institute of Medical and Veterinary Science (Aust.)
In *Chem.* indium
in. inch
inbd. inboard
Inc. Incorporated
inc. 1. included 2. including
3. inclusive 4. income 5. incomplete
6. increase
incept. inceptive
incl. 1. including 2. inclusive
incog. incognito
incor. incorporated
incr. 1. increase 2. increased
3. increasing
IND 1. *IVR* India 2. *in nomine Dei* (*L.* in God's name)

Ind.   **1.** Independent   **2.** India(n)
   3. Indiana   **4.** Indies
ind.   **1.** independence   **2.** independent
   3. index   **4.** indicative   **5.** indigo
   6. indirect   **7.** industrial   **8.** industry
indef.   indefinite
indic.   **1.** indicating   **2.** indicative
   3. indicator
individ.   individual
induc.   induction
Inf.   Infantry
inf.   **1.** inferior   **2.** infinitive   **3.** influence
   4. information   **5.** *infra* (*L.* below)
infin.   infinitive
infl.   influence(d)
init.   **1.** initial   **2.** *initio* (*L.* in the
   beginning)
in loc. cit.   *in loco citato* (*L.* in the place
   cited)
inorg.   inorganic
INRI   *Iesus Nazarenus Rex Iudaeorum* (*L.*
   Jesus of Nazareth, King of the Jews)
INS   International News Service
ins.   **1.** inches   **2.** inspector   **3.** insulated
   4. insulation   **5.** insurance
insp.   **1.** inspected   **2.** inspector
Inst.   Institute
inst.   **1.** instant   **2.** instantaneous
   3. instrumental
InstAct   Institute of Actuaries

InstCE Institution of Civil Engineers
InstD Institute of Directors
InstEE Institution of Electrical Engineers
InstF Institute of Fuel
InstGasE Institution of Gas Engineers
InstHE Institution of Highway Engineers
InstME Institute of Marine Engineers
InstMechE Institution of Mechanical Engineers
InstMet Institute of Metals
InstMM Institution of Mining and Metallurgy
Instn. Institution
InstP Institute of Physics
InstPet Institute of Petroleum
instr. 1. instructor 2. instrument(al)
InstWE Institution of Water Engineers
int. 1. interest 2. interim 3. interior 4. interjection 5. internal 6. international 7. interpreter 8. intransitive
intens. 1. intensified 2. intensive
inter. intermediate
interj. interjection
internat. international
INTERPOL (in'tər pol') International Criminal Police Commission
interrog. 1. interrogation 2. interrogative
intl. international

intr., intrans.   intransitive
in trans.   *in transitu* (*L.* on the way)
Int. Rev.   Internal Revenue (US)
intro.   **1.** introduction **2.** introductory
INucE   Institution of Nuclear Engineers
inv.   **1.** invented **2.** invention
   3. inventor **4.** invoice
invt.   inventory
I/O   *DP* input/output
Io   *Chem.* ionium
Io.   Iowa
IOB   **1.** Institute of Bankers **2.** Institute
   of Bookkeepers **3.** Institute of Builders
IOBI   Institute of Bankers in Ireland
IOBS   Institute of Bankers in Scotland
IOC   **1.** Institute of Chemistry
   2. International Olympic Committee
IOF   **1.** Independent Order of Foresters
   2. Institute of Fuel
IOGT   Independent Order of Good
   Templars
IOM   **1.** Institute of Office Management
   2. Isle of Man
IOOF   Independent Order of Odd Fellows
IOP   **1.** Institute of Petroleum **2.** Institute
   of Physics **3.** Institute of Printing
IOR   Independent Order of Rechabites
IOU   I owe you
IOW   Isle of Wight
IPA   **1.** Institute of Practitioners in

Advertising **2.** Institute of Public
Administration **3.** International Phonetic
Alphabet *or* Association **4.** International
Publishers' Association

IPBM interplanetary ballistic missile
IPCS Institution of Professional Civil
Servants
IPE **1.** Institution of Plant Engineers
2. Institution of Production Engineers
IPHE Institution of Public Health
Engineers
IPI International Press Institute
IPM Institute of Personnel Management
IPR Institute of Public Relations
IProdE Institution of Production
Engineers
ips inches per second
IQ **1.** Institute of Quarrying
2. intelligence quotient
i.q. *idem quod* (*L.* the same as)
IQS Institute of Quantity Surveyors
IR **1.** infrared **2.** Inland Revenue **3.** *IVR*
Iran
Ir *Chem.* iridium
Ir. **1.** Ireland **2.** Irish
IRA **1.** Institute of Registered Architects
2. Irish Republican Army
Iran. Iranian
IRB Irish Republican Brotherhood
IRBM intermediate range ballistic missile

IRC International Red Cross
IRE Institute of Radio Engineers (US)
Ire. Ireland
IRL *IVR* Republic of Ireland
IRN Independent Radio News
IRO **1.** Inland Revenue Office
 2. International Refugees Organization
IRQ *IVR* Iraq
irreg. irregular(ly)
IRS Internal Revenue Service (US)
IRSF Inland Revenue Staff Federation
IRTE Institute of Road Transport
Engineers
IS *IVR* Iceland
Is. **1.** *Bib.* Isaiah **2.** Island **3.** Isle
ISBN International Standard Book
Number
ISCh Incorporated Society of Chiropodists
ISE Institution of Structural Engineers
ISF International Shipping Federation
ISFA Institute of Shipping and
Forwarding Agents
ISI Iron and Steel Institute
isl. **1.** island **2.** isle
ISM Imperial Service Medal
ISO **1.** Imperial Service Order
 2. International Standardization
Organization
ISPCC Irish Society for the Prevention of
Cruelty to Children

IST

IST Institute of Science and Technology
ISTC Iron and Steel Trades Confederation
isth. isthmus
It. 1. Italian 2. Italic 3. Italy
ITA 1. Independent Television Authority
2. Initial Teaching Alphabet
Ital. 1. Italian 2. Italic
ITB Irish Tourish Board
ITN Independent Television News
ITO International Trade Organization
ITU International Telecommunications Union
ITV Independent Television
IU 1. immunising unit 2. international unit
IUD intra-uterine device
IUPAC International Union of Pure and Applied Chemistry
IUPAP International Union of Pure and Applied Physics
i.v. 1. initial velocity 2. intravenous
IVB Invalidity Benefit
IVR International Vehicle Registration
IVS International Voluntary Service
IW Isle of Wight
IWE Institution of Water Engineers
IWG Imperial Wire Gauge
IWM Institution of Works Managers
IWW Industrial Workers of the World (US)

J

J 1. *IVR* Japan 2. *Phys.* joule
   3. Journal 4. Judge 5. Justice
j *Eng.* $\sqrt{-1}$
JA 1. *IVR* Jamaica 2. Joint Account
   3. Judge Advocate
Ja. January
JAEC Joint Atomic Energy Committee
   (US)
JAG Judge Advocate General
Jam. 1. Jamaica 2. *Bib.* James
Jan. January
Jap. Japan(ese)
Jas. James
JATO (jā′tō) jet-assisted take-off
Jav. Javanese
JB *Jurum Baccalaureus* (*L.* Bachelor of
   Laws)
JC 1. Jesus Christ 2. Jockey Club
   3. Julius Caesar 4. Jurisconsult
   5. Justice Clerk 6. Juvenile Court
JCB 1. *Juris Canonici Baccalaureus* (*L.*
   Bachelor of Canon Law) 2. *Juris Civilis
   Baccalaureus* (*L.* Bachelor of Civil Law)
JCD 1. *Juris Canonici Doctor* (*L.* Doctor
   of Canon Law) 2. *Juris Civilis Doctor* (*L.*
   Doctor of Civil Law)

JCL 1. *Juris Canonici Licentiatus* (*L.* Licentiate in Canon Law) 2. *Juris Civilis Licentiatus* (*L.* Licentiate in Civil Law) 3. *DP* job control language

JCR Junior Common Room

JCS Joint Chiefs of Staff

jct. junction

JD 1. *Jurum Doctor* (*L.* Doctor of Jurisprudence) 2. juvenile delinquent

Je. June

Jer. 1. *Bib.* Jeremiah 2. Jerusalem

j.g. junior grade

JHS *Jesus Hominum Salvator* (*L.* Jesus Saviour of Men)

JI Institute of Journalists

JJ 1. Judges 2. Justices

Jl. July

Jnr. Junior

Jos. 1. Joseph 2. Josiah

Josh. *Bib.* Joshua

jour. 1. journal 2. journalist 3. journeyman

JP 1. jet propulsion 2. Justice of the Peace

Jpn. Japan(ese)

Jr. Junior

JSD *Jurum Scientiae Doctor* (*L.* Doctor of Juristic Science)

jt. joint

Ju. June

JUD *Juris utriusque Doctor* (*L.* Doctor of Canon and Civil Law)
Jud. *Bib.* Judith
Judg. *Bib.* Judges
Jul. July
Jun. 1. June 2. Junior
junc. junction
Junr. Junior
JurD *Juris Doctor* (*L.* Doctor of Law)
jurisp. jurisprudence
Jus. Justice
juv. juvenile
Jy. July

K

K 1. *Elec.* capacity 2. *symbol for* carat
3. *Math.* constant 4. *Phys.* kaon 5. *Phys.*
kelvin 6. *IVR* Khmer Republic 7. kilo
8. King 9. knight 10. knit 11. kopeck
12. *Chem.* potassium 13. *Met.* smoke
KA Knight of the Order of St Andrew
ka. kathode (US)
KADU (kä′dŏŏ) Kenya African Democratic Union
Kan., Kans. Kansas

KANU (kä'nōō)   Kenya African National Union

KAR   King's African Rifles

Kas.   Kansas

KB   1. King's Bench   2. King's Bishop
3. Knight Bachelor   4. Knight of the Order of the Bath

kb   kilobar

KBE   Knight of the Order of the British Empire

KBP   King's Bishop's Pawn

KC   1. Kennel Club   2. King's College
3. King's Counsel   4. Knight Commander
5. Knight of Columbus

kc   kilocycle

KCB   Knight Commander of the Order of the Bath

KCH   Knight Commander of Hanover

KCHS   Knight Commander of the Order of the Holy Sepulchre

kCi.   kilocurie

KCIE   Knight Commander of the Order of the Indian Empire

KCMG   Knight Commander of the Order of St Michael and St George

KCSI   Knight Commander of the Order of the Star of India

KCVO   Knight Commander of the Royal Victorian Order

k.d.   knocked down

KE kinetic energy

Ken. Kentucky

keV kilo-electronvolt

KG Knight of the Order of the Garter

kg 1. keg 2. kilogram

KGB *Komitet Gosudarstvennoi Bezopasnosti* (*Russ.* Committee of State Security, USSR)

KGC Knight of the Golden Circle (US)

KGCB Knight of the Grand Cross of the Order of the Bath

KGF Knight of the Order of the Golden Fleece

Kgs. *Bib.* Kings

kHz kilohertz

KIA killed in action

kilo kilogram

kJ kilojoule

KJV King James Version (of the Bible)

KKK Ku Klux Klan

KKt King's Knight

KKtP King's Knight's Pawn

kl kilolitre

KLH Knight of the Legion of Honour

KLM *Koninklije Luchtvaart Maatschappij* (Royal Dutch Airlines)

KM 1. King's Medal 2. Knight of Malta

km kilometre

km/h kilometres per hour

kn *Naut.* knot

KN King's Knight
KNP King's Knight's Pawn
Knt. Knight
KO knock-out
K of C Knight of Columbus
K of L Knight of Labour
K of P Knight of Pythias
KOSB King's Own Scottish Borderers
KOYLI King's Own Yorkshire Light Infantry
KP 1. King's Pawn 2. Knight of Pythias 3. Knight of the Order of St Patrick
KPM King's Police Medal
KR King's Rook
Kr *Chem.* krypton
kr. 1. kreutzer 2. krone
KRC Knight of the Red Cross
KRP King's Rook's Pawn
KS King's Scholar
KSG Knight of the Order of St George
KSI Knight of the Star of India
KStJ Knight Commander of the Order of St John of Jerusalem
KT 1. Knight of the Order of the Thistle 2. Knight Templar
Kt. Knight
kt. 1. karat 2. kiloton 3. *Naut.* knot
Kt. Bach. Knight Bachelor
kV kilovolt
kW kilowatt

kWh kilowatt-hour
KWIC (kwik) *DP* keyword in context
KWOC (kwok) *DP* keyword out of context
KWT *IVR* Kuwait
Ky. Kentucky

L

L **1.** *Elec.* inductance **2.** Lake **3.** *Phys.* latent heat **4.** Latin **5.** learner driver **6.** Liberal **7.** Licentiate **8.** Lodge **9.** longitude **10.** *IVR* Luxembourg **11.** *Roman numeral for* 50
l litre
l. **1.** lake **2.** land **3.** latitude **4.** law **5.** leaf **6.** league **7.** left **8.** length **9.** *liber* (*L.* book) **10.** *libra* (*L.* pound) **11.** line **12.** link **13.** lire **14.** low
LA **1.** Law Agent **2.** Legislative Assembly **3.** Library Association **4.** Literate in Arts **5.** Los Angeles
La *Chem.* lanthanum
La. Louisiana
LAA Library Association of Australia
Lab. **1.** Labour **2.** Labrador

lab. **1.** labial **2.** labiate **3.** laboratory
  4. labour(er)
LAC **1.** Leading Aircraftman
  2. Licentiate of the Apothecaries' Company
LACW Leading Aircraftwoman
LAE London Association of Engineers
LAFTA (laf'tə) Latin American Free Trade
  Association
Lam. *Bib.* Lamentations
lam. laminated
LAMDA (lam'də) London Academy of
  Music and Dramatic Art
Lancs. Lancashire
lang. language
LAO **1.** *IVR* Laos **2.** Licentiate in
  Obstetrics
LAR *IVR* Libya
LAS **1.** Land Agents' Society **2.** League
  of Arab States **3.** Lord Advocate of
  Scotland
Lat. Latin
lat. latitude
LB **1.** *IVR* Liberia **2.** *Litterarum
  Baccalaureus* (*L.* Bachelor of Letters)
  3. Local Board
lb. pound
l.b.w. *Cricket* leg before wicket
LC **1.** Lance Corporal **2.** Library of
  Congress (US) **3.** Lord Chamberlain
L/C Letter of Credit

l.c. **1.** left centre **2.** *loco citato* (*L.* in the place cited) **3.** *Ptg.* lower case
LCB Lord Chief Baron
LCC **1.** London Chamber of Commerce **2.** London County Council
LCD lowest common denominator
LCE Licentiate in Civil Engineering
LCh *Licentiatus Chirurgiae* (*L.* Licentiate in Surgery)
LCJ Lord Chief Justice
LCL Licentiate of Civil Law
LCM **1.** London College of Music **2.** lowest common multiple
LCP Licentiate of the College of Preceptors
L/Cpl Lance Corporal
LCT **1.** landing craft tank **2.** local civil time
LD **1.** Lady Day **2.** lethal dose **3.** Licentiate in Divinity
Ld. Lord
ld. **1.** lead **2.** load
Ldg. Leading
Ldp. Lordship
LDS **1.** Latter-Day Saints **2.** *Laus Deo semper* (*L.* praise be to God always) **3.** Licentiate in Dental Surgery
LDV Local Defence Volunteers (later **HG**)
LEA Local Education Authority
lea. **1.** league **2.** leather

lect. lecture(r)
LED light-emitting diode
leg. 1. legal 2. legate 3. *Mus. legato* (*It.* smooth)
legis. 1. legislation 2. legislative 3. legislature
Leics. Leicestershire
LEM lunar excursion module
LEPRA (lep′rə) British Leprosy Relief Association
Lett. Lettish
LEV lunar excursion vehicle
Lev. *Bib.* Leviticus
lex. lexicon
lexicog. 1. lexicographical 2. lexicographer 3. lexicography
LF low frequency
l.f. *Ptg.* light face
LFPS Licentiate of the Faculty of Physicians and Surgeons
LG 1. Life Guards 2. Low German
lg. large
LGSM Licentiate of the Guildhall School of Music
lgth. length
lg. tn. long ton
LGU Ladies' Golf Union
LH 1. Legion of Honour 2. luteinizing hormone
l.h. left hand

LHA Lord High Admiral
LHC Lord High Commissioner
LHD *Litterarum Humaniorum Doctor* (*L.* Doctor of Humane Letters)
l.h.d. left hand drive
LHT Lord High Treasurer
LI **1.** Light Infantry **2.** Long Island
Li *Chem.* lithium
Lib. **1.** Liberal **2.** Liberia
lib. **1.** *liber* (*L.* book) **2.** librarian **3.** library
Lic. Med. Licentiate in Medicine
Lieut. Lieutenant
lin. **1.** lineal **2.** linear
Lincs. Lincolnshire
ling. linguistics
liq. **1.** liquid **2.** liquor
lit. **1.** literal **2.** literary **3.** literature **4.** litre
LitD *Litterarum Doctor* (*L.* Doctor of Letters)
Lith. Lithuania(n)
lith., litho lithograph(y)
lithol. lithology
LittB *Litterarum Baccalaureus* (*L.* Bachelor of Letters)
LittD *Litterarum Doctor* (*L.* Doctor of Letters)
LittM *Litterarum Magister* (*L.* Master of Letters)

LJ Lord Justice
LL Lord Lieutenant
ll. lines
LL.B. *Legum Baccalaureus* (*L.* Bachelor of Laws)
LLCM Licentiate of the London College of Music
LL.D. *Legum Doctor* (*L.* Doctor of Laws)
LLI Lord Lieutenant of Ireland
LL.L. Licentiate in Laws
LL.M. *Legum Magister* (*L.* Master of Laws)
LM **1.** Licentiate in Medicine **2.** Licentiate in Midwifery **3.** Licentiate in Music **4.** *Mus.* long metre **5.** Lord Mayor **6.** lunar module
lm *Phys.* lumen
LMed Licentiate in Medicine
LMS **1.** London Mathematical Society **2.** London Missionary Society
LMT local mean time
LMus Licentiate of Music
LN League of Nations
ln *Math.* natural logarithm
LNG liquefied natural gas
LOA leave of absence
LOC Library of Congress (US)
loc. cit. *loco citato* (*L.* in the place cited)
log logarithm
log. logic

long.   longitude
LOOM   Loyal Order of Moose (US)
loq.   *loquitur* (*L.* he/she speaks)
LOS   line of sight
LP   **1.** Labour Party **2.** long-playing (record) **3.** Lord Provost **4.** Low Pressure
LPG   liquefied petroleum gas
LPh   Licentiate of Philosophy
LPN   Licensed Practical Nurse (US)
L'pool   Liverpool
LPS   Lord Privy Seal
LR   Lloyd's Register
Lr   *Chem.* lawrencium
LRAD   Licentiate of the Royal Academy of Dancing
LRAM   Licentiate of the Royal Academy of Music
LRBM   long range ballistic missile
LRCM   Licentiate of the Royal College of Music
LRCP   Licentiate of the Royal College of Physicians
LRCS   Licentiate of the Royal College of Surgeons
LRCVS   Licentiate of the Royal College of Veterinary Surgeons
LRFPS   Licentiate of the Royal Faculty of Physicians and Surgeons
LRIBA   Licentiate of the Royal Institute of British Architects

LRS Lloyd's Register of Shipping
LS 1. Law Society 2. Leading Seaman
3. *IVR* Lesotho 4. Licentiate in Surgery
5. *loco sigilla* (*L.* place of the seal)
l.s. left side
LSA 1. Licentiate of Science in
Agriculture 2. Licentiate of the Society of
Apothecaries
LSD 1. *librae, solidi, denarii* (*L.* pounds,
shillings, pence) 2. lysergic acid
diethylamide
LSE 1. London School of Economics
2. London Stock Exchange
LSNSW Linnean Society of New South
Wales
LSNY Linnean Society of New York
LSO London Symphony Orchestra
LSS Life Saving Service (US)
LST 1. Licentiate in Sacred Theology
2. Local Standard Time (US)
LT *Elec.* low tension
Lt. Lieutenant
l.t. 1. local time 2. long ton (US)
LTA Lawn Tennis Association
Lt. Col. Lieutenant Colonel
Lt. Comdr. Lieutenant Commander
Ltd. Limited
Lt. Gen. Lieutenant General
Lt. Gov. Lieutenant Governor
LTh Licentiate in Theology

LTM Licentiate in Tropical Medicine
Lu *Chem.* lutetium
Luth. Lutheran
Lux. Luxembourg
LV luncheon voucher
lv. **1.** leave **2.** livre
LVN Licensed Vocational Nurse (US)
LW **1.** left wing **2.** long wave **3.** low water
Lw *Chem.* lawrencium
LWM low water mark
lx *Phys.* lux
LXX *Bib.* Septuagint

M

M **1.** mach (number) **2.** Majesty
3. *IVR* Malta **4.** Manitoba **5.** Marquis
6. Master **7.** *Phys.* maxwell **8.** Medieval
9. Member **10.** *Mus. mezzo* (*It.* half)
11. Middle **12.** Monday **13.** *Monsieur*
14. motorway **15.** Mountain **16.** *Roman numeral for* 1 000
m **1.** *Phys.* mass **2.** metre
m. **1.** male **2.** manual **3.** mark
4. married **5.** masculine **6.** medium
7. meridian **8.** mile **9.** mill **10.** million

11. minim **12.** minute **13.** modulus
14. month **15.** moon **16.** morning

MA **1.** *Magister Artium* (*L.* Master of Arts) **2.** mental age **3.** Middle Ages **4.** Military Academy **5.** *IVR* Morocco

mA milliampere

MAA Master-At-Arms

MAAG Military Assistance Advisory Group

MAArch Master of Arts in Architecture

MAAS Member of the American Academy of Arts and Sciences

MABE Master of Agricultural Business and Economics

Mac., Macc. *Bib.* Maccabees

Maced. Macedonia(n)

mach. **1.** machine **2.** machinery **3.** machinist

MACS Member of the American Chemical Society

MAE **1.** Master of Aeronautical Engineering **2.** Master of Arts in Education

MAEd Master of Arts in Education

mag. **1.** magazine **2.** magnetic **3.** magnetism **4.** magnesium **5.** magneto **6.** magnitude

MAgEc Master of Agricultural Economics

MAgEd Master of Agricultural Education

MAgr Master of Agriculture

MAI *Magister in Arte Ingeniaria* (*L.* Master of Engineering)

MAIChE Member of the American Institute of Chemical Engineers

MAIEE Member of the American Institute of Electrical Engineers

MAIME Member of the American Institute of Mining and Metallurgical Engineers

Maj. Major

Maj. Gen. Major General

MAL *IVR* Malaysia

Mal. 1. *Bib.* Malachi 2. Malay(an)

MALD Master of Arts in Law and Diplomacy

MALS 1. Master of Arts in Liberal Studies 2. Master of Arts in Library Science

Man. 1. Manila 2. Manitoba

man. manual

manuf. 1. manufacture 2. manufacturing

MAO *Chem.* monoamine oxidase

MAR Master of Arts in Religion

Mar. March

mar. 1. marine 2. maritime 3. married

MArch Master of Architecture

March. Marchioness

marg. margin(al)

Marq. 1. Marquess 2. Marquis

masc. masculine
MASH (mash) Mobile Army Surgical Hospital (US)
Mass. Massachusetts
MAT Master of Arts in Teaching
mat. 1. matinee 2. maturity
math. 1. mathematical 2. mathematician 3. mathematics
MATS (mats) Military Air Transport Service (US)
Matt. *Bib.* Matthew
max. maximum
MB *Medicinae Baccalaureus* (*L.* Bachelor of Medicine)
mb millibar
MBA Master of Business Administration
MBE Member of the Order of the British Empire
MBIM Member of the British Institute of Management
MBS Mutual Broadcasting System (US)
MC 1. Master Commandant 2. Master of Ceremonies 3. Medical Corps 4. Member of Congress 5. Military Cross 6. *IVR* Monaco
mc 1. megacycle 2. millicurie
MCC Marylebone Cricket Club
MCE Master of Civil Engineering
MCh *Magister Chirurgiae* (*L.* Master of Surgery)

MChD *Magister Chirurgiae Dentalis* (*L.* Master of Dental Surgery)

MChE Master of Chemical Engineering

MCL Master of Civil Law

MCom Master of Commerce

MCP 1. male chauvanist pig 2. Member of the College of Preceptors

MCS 1. Master of Commercial Science 2. Master of Computer Science 3. missile control system

Mc/s megacycles per second

MD 1. Managing Director 2. Medical Department 3. *Medicinae Doctor* (*L.* Doctor of Medicine) 4. mentally deficient

Md *Chem.* mendelivium

Md. Maryland

MDiv Master of Divinity

Mdlle. *Mademoiselle*

Mdm. Madam

Mdme. *Madame*

MDS Master of Dental Surgery

MDSc Master of Dental Science

mdse. merchandise

MDT Mountain Daylight Time (US)

MDV Doctor of Veterinary Medicine

ME 1. Master of Education 2. Mechanical Engineer 3. Medical Examiner 4. Methodist Episcopal 5. Military Engineer 6. Mining Engineer 7. Most Excellent

Me *Chem.* methyl
Me. Maine
MEA Master of Engineering Administration
meas. measure
MEC 1. Master of Engineering Chemistry 2. Member of the Executive Council
mech. 1. mechanical 2. mechanics 3. mechanism
MEcon Master of Economics
MEd Master of Education
med. 1. medical 2. medicine 3. medieval 4. medium
Medit. Mediterranean
MEF Middle East Forces
meg megohm
mem. 1. member 2. *memento* (*L.* remember) 3. memoir 4. memorandum 5. memorial
MEng Master of Engineering
MEP 1. Master of Engineering Physics 2. Member of the European Parliament
mep mean effective pressure
MEPA Master of Engineering and Public Administration
meq. milliequivalent
mer. meridian
merc. 1. mercantile 2. mercurial 3. mercury

met. 1. metaphor 2. metaphysics
  3. meteorological 4. meteorology
  5. metropolitan
metal. 1. metallurgical 2. metallurgy
metaph. 1. metaphor 2. metaphysics
meteor. 1. meteorological
  2. meteorology
Meth. Methodist
MeV 1. mega-electron-volt 2. million
  electron–volts
MEX *IVR* Mexico
Mex. 1. Mexican 2. Mexico
MF 1. machine finish 2. medium
  frequency
mf 1. *Mus. mezzo forte* (*It.* moderately
  loud) 2. millifarad
MFA Master of Fine Arts (US)
mfd. manufactured
mfg. manufacturing
MFH Master of Fox Hounds
mfr. manufacture(r)
MFS 1. Master of Food Science
  2. Master of Foreign Study
MFT Master of Foreign Trade
mfv motor fleet vessel
MG 1. machine gun 2. Military
  Government
Mg 1. *Chem.* magnesium 2. megagram
mg milligram
MGB motor gun boat

Mgr. 1. Manager 2. *Monseigneur*
3. *Monsignor*
mgt. management
MH Medal of Honour
mh millihenry
MHA Master of Hospital Administration
MHCI Member of the Hotel and Catering Institute
MHD magnetohydrodynamics
MHE Master of Home Economics
MHF medium high frequency
MHG Middle High German
MHK Member of the House of Keys
MHL Master of Hebrew Literature
MHLG Ministry of Housing and Local Government
MHR Member of the House of Representatives (US)
MHz megahertz
MI 1. Military Intelligence 2. Mounted Infantry
mi. 1. mile 2. mill
MIA 1. Master of International Affairs 2. missing in action
MIAE Member of the Institution of Automobile Engineers
MIAeE Member of the Institute of Aeronautical Engineers
MIAM Member of the Institute of Advanced Motorists

MIBE   Member of the Institution of British Engineers

Mic.   *Bib.* Micah

MICA   Member of the Institute of Chartered Accountants of England and Wales

Mich.   1. Michaelmas   2. Michigan

MIChemE   Member of the Institution of Chemical Engineers

MICR   *DP* magnetic ink character recognition

Mid.   Midshipman

mid.   1. middle   2. midnight

MIDAS (mī′dəs)   Missile Defence Alarm System

Middx.   Middlesex (former county)

MIE   1. Master of Industrial Engineering   2. Master of Irrigation Engineering

MIEE   Member of the Institution of Electrical Engineers

MIFE   Member of the Institution of Fire Engineers

MIGE   Member of the Institution of Gas Engineers

MIHVE   Member of the Institution of Heating and Ventilating Engineers

MIIE   Member of the Institution of Industrial Engineers

mil   millilitre

mil.   1. military   2. militia

MILocoE Member of the Institution of Locomotive Engineers
MILR Master of Industrial and Labor Relations (US)
MIMarE Member of the Institute of Marine Engineers
MIMechE Member of the Institution of Mechanical Engineers
MIMI Member of the Institute of the Motor Industry
MIMinE Member of the Institution of Mining Engineers
MIMM Member of the Institution of Mining and Metallurgy
MIMunE Member of the Institution of Municipal Engineers
MIN Member of the Institute of Navigation
Min. Ministry
min. 1. mineralogical 2. mineralogy 3. minim 4. minimum 5. mining 6. minister 7. minor 8. minute
MIND (mīnd) National Association for Mental Health
mineral. 1. mineralogical 2. mineralogy
Minn. Minnesota
MInstMet Member of the Institute of Metals
MInstMM Member of the Institution of Mining and Metallurgy

MInstT   Member of the Institute of Transport

MInstWE   Member of the Institution of Water Engineers

MINucE   Member of the Institution of Nuclear Engineers

MIPet   Member of the Institute of Petroleum

MIPHE   Member of the Institution of Public Health Engineers

MIPlantE   Member of the Institution of Plant Engineers

MIPR   Member of the Institute of Public Relations

MIProdE   Member of the Institution of Production Engineers

MIQ   Member of the Institute of Quarrying

MIRA   Member of the Institute of Registered Architects

MIRE   Member of the Institution of Radio Engineers

MIRV   multiple independently targeted re-entry vehicle

MIS   **1.** Master of International Service **2.** Mining Institute of Scotland

misc.   **1.** miscellaneous **2.** miscellany

Miss.   Mississippi

miss.   mission(ary)

MIStructE   Member of the Institution of Structural Engineers

MIT Massachusetts Institute of Technology

MITI Ministry for International Trade and Industry

MIWE Member of the Institution of Water Engineers

MJ 1. Master of Journalism 2. Master of Jurisprudence 3. megajoule 4. Ministry of Justice

MJI Member of the Institute of Journalists

mk. mark

mks metre-kilogram-second

mkt. market

ML 1. Master of Law 2. Master of Letters 3. *Medicinae Licentiatus* (*L.* Licentiate in Medicine) 4. Ministry of Labour

ml 1. mail 2. mile 3. millilitre

MLA 1. Master of Landscape Architecture 2. Member of the Legislative Assembly 3. Modern Language Association (US)

MLB Maritime Labor Board (US)

MLC Member of the Legislative Council

MLD minimum lethal dose

MLF multilateral force

MLitt *Magister Litterarum* (*L.* Master of Letters)

Mlle. *Mademoiselle*

MLR *Fin.* minimum lending rate

MLS **1.** Master of Library Science
2. Member of the Linnean Society
MM **1.** Master Mason **2.** Master of
Music **3.** *Messieurs* **4.** Military Medal
5. Their Majesties
mm **1.** *millia* (*L.* thousand) **2.** millimetre
MMB Milk Marketing Board
MME **1.** Master of Mechanical
Engineering **2.** Master of Mining
Engineering
Mme. *Madame*
Mmes. *Mesdames*
mmf magnetomotive force
MMS Methodist Missionary Society
MMSc Master of Medical Science
MMus Master of Music
MN Merchant Navy
Mn *Chem.* manganese
MNA Master of Nursing Administration
MNAOA Merchant Navy and Airline
Officers' Association
MNAS Member of the National Academy
of Sciences (US)
MNE Master of Nuclear Engineering
MNS Master of Nutritional Science
MO **1.** Mail Order **2.** Medical Officer
3. *modus operandi* (*L.* mode of operation)
4. Money Order
Mo *Chem.* molybdenum
Mo. **1.** Missouri **2.** Monday

mo. month
MOA Ministry of Aviation
MOC Mother of the Chapel (printing unions)
MOD Ministry of Defence
mod. 1. moderate 2. modern 3. modulus
MOE Ministry of Education
MOH 1. Medical Officer of Health 2. Ministry of Health
Moham. Mohammedan
MOI 1. Ministry of Information 2. Ministry of the Interior
MOIG Master of Occupational Information and Guidance
MOL manned orbiting laboratory
mol *Chem.* mole
mol. 1. molecular 2. molecule
mol. wt. molecular weight
Mon. 1. Monastery 2. Monday 3. Monmouthshire (former county) 4. *Monseigneur* 5. *Monsignor*
mon. 1. monastery 2. monetary
Mong. Mongolia(n)
Mons. *Monsieur*
Mont. 1. Montana 2. Montgomeryshire (former county)
MOpt Master of Optometry
Mor. Morocco
morph. 1. morphological 2. morphology

mos.　months
MOT　Ministry of Transport
MP　1. Member of Parliament
2. Metropolitan Police　3. Military Police
4. Mounted Police　5. Municipal Police
(US)
mp　*Mus. mezzo piano* (*It.* moderately
soft)
m.p.　melting point
MPA　1. Master of Professional
Accounting　2. Master of Public
Administration　3. Master of Public Affairs
MPBW　Ministry of Public Buildings and
Works
MPE　Master of Physical Education
mpg　miles per gallon
MPH　Master of Public Health
MPh　Master of Philosophy
mph　miles per hour
MPharm　Master of Pharmacy
MPhil　Master of Philosophy
MPL　Master of Patent Law
MPNI　Ministry of Pensions and National
Insurance
MPP　Member of Provincial Parliament
(Can.)
MPS　1. Member of the Pharmaceutical
Society　2. Member of the Philological
Society　3. Member of the Physical Society

MR 1. Master of the Rolls
2. motivational research
Mr. Mister
MRA Moral Rearmament
MRAC Member of the Royal Agricultural College
MRACP Member of the Royal Australasian College of Physicians
MRAeS Member of the Royal Aeronautical Society
MRAIC Member of the Royal Architectural Institute of Canada
MRAS 1. Member of the Royal Academy of Science 2. Member of the Royal Astronomical Society
MRBM medium range ballistic missile
MRC Medical Research Council
MRCA multi-role combat aircraft
MRCC Member of the Royal College of Chemistry
MRCOG Member of the Royal College of Obstetricians and Gynaecologists
MRCP 1. Member of the Royal College of Physicians 2. Member of the Royal College of Preceptors
MRCS Member of the Royal College of Surgeons
MRCVS Member of the Royal College of Veterinary Surgeons
MRE Master of Religious Education

MRGS   Member of the Royal Geographical Society

MRH   Member of the Royal Household

MRI   Member of the Royal Institution

MRIA   Member of the Royal Irish Academy

MRIC   Member of the Royal Institute of Chemistry

MRICS   Member of the Royal Institution of Chartered Surveyors

MRINA   Member of the Royal Institution of Naval Architects

MRP   1. Manufacturer's Recommended Price 2. Master of Regional Planning

MRSH   Member of the Royal Society of Health

MRSL   Member of the Royal Society of Literature

MRSM   1. Member of the Royal Society of Medicine 2. Member of the Royal Society of Musicians

MRSPP   Member of the Royal Society of Portrait Painters

MRST   Member of the Royal Society of Teachers

MS   1. manuscript 2. Master of Science 3. Master of Surgery 4. *IVR* Mauritius 5. *memoriae sacrum* (*L.* sacred to the memory of) 6. motor ship 7. multiple sclerosis

ms   millisecond
m/s   metres per second
MSA   Mutual Security Agency (US)
MSA, MSAgr   Master of Science in Agriculture
MSAE   **1.** Master of Science in Aeronautical Engineering **2.** Member of the Society of Automotive Engineers (US)
MSAM   Master of Science in Applied Mechanics
MSArch   Master of Science in Architecture
MSBA   Master of Science in Business Administration
MSBC   Master of Science in Building Construction
MSBus   Master of Science in Business
MSC   Manpower Services Commission
MSc   Master of Science
MScD   **1.** Doctor of Medical Science (US) **2.** Master of Dental Science
MSCE   Master of Science in Civil Engineering
MSChE   Master of Science in Chemical Engineering
MSCP   Master of Science in Community Planning
MSD   **1.** Doctor of Medical Science **2.** Master of Science in Dentistry

MSE **1.** Master of Science in Education
2. Master of Science in Engineering
msec millisecond
MSEd Master of Science in Education
MSEE Master of Science in Electrical Engineering
MSEM Master of Science in Engineering Mechanics
MSF medium standard frequency
MSG *Chem.* monosodium glutamate
MSGM Master of Science in Government Management
Msgr. **1.** *Monseigneur* **2.** *Monsignor*
MSHA Master of Science in Hospital Administration
MSHE Master of Science in Home Economics
MSHort Master of Science in Horticulture
MSHyg Master of Science in Hygiene
MSIE Master of Science in Industrial Engineering
MSJ Master of Science in Journalism
MSL Master of Science in Linguistics
msl mean sea level
MSM **1.** Master of Sacred Music
2. Master of Science in Music
MSME Master of Science in Mechanical Engineering
MSMetE Master of Science in Metallurgical Engineering

MSMgtE Master of Science in Management Engineering
MSN Master of Science in Nursing
MSPE Master of Science in Physical Education
MSPH Master of Science in Public Health
MSPhar Master of Science in Pharmacy
MSPHE Master of Science in Public Health Engineering
MSS Master of Social Science
MST 1. Master of Science in Teaching 2. Mountain Standard Time (US)
MSTS Military Sea Transportation Service (US)
MSW Master of Social Work
MT 1. Masoretic Text 2. mean time 3. mechanical transport
Mt. Mount(ain)
m.t. metric tonne
MTB motor torpedo boat
MTech Master of Technology
mtg. 1. meeting 2. mortgage
MTh Master of Theology
mth month
MTI moving target indicator
mtn. mountain
Mt. Rev. Most Reverend
MU Musicians' Union
mun. municipal

mus.   **1.** museum   **2.** music   **3.** musical   **4.** musician

MusB, MusBac   *Musicae Baccalaureus* (*L.* Bachelor of Music)

MusD, MusDoc   *Musicae Doctor* (*L.* Doctor of Music)

MusM   *Musicae Magister* (*L.* Master of Music)

mut.   **1.** mutilated   **2.** mutual

mV   millivolt

m.v.   **1.** market value   **2.** mean variation **3.** *Mus. mezza voce* (*It.* half the power of voice)   **4.** motor vessel   **5.** muzzle velocity

MVA   megavolt-ampere

MVD   Doctor of Veterinary Medicine

MVO   Member of the Royal Victorian Order

MVS   **1.** Master of Veterinary Science **2.** Master of Veterinary Surgery

MW   **1.** *IVR* Malawi   **2.** medium wave **3.** megawatt

mW   milliwatt

MWPA   Married Women's Property Act

Mx.   Middlesex (former county)

MY   motor yacht

mycol.   **1.** mycological   **2.** mycology

myg   myriagram (US)

myl   myrialitre (US)

mym   myriametre (US)

myth.   **1.** mythological   **2.** mythology

N

N

N **1.** *Chess* knight **2.** National
  3. Nationalist **4.** Navy **5.** *Phys.* newton
  6. *Chem.* nitrogen **7.** Noon **8.** Norse
  9. North **10.** *IVR* Norway **11.** November

n. **1.** nail **2.** name **3.** *natus* (*L.* born)
  4. navy **5.** nephew **6.** net **7.** neuter
  8. *Phys.* neutron **9.** new **10.** nominative
  11. noon **12.** note **13.** noun
  14. number

NA **1.** National Academician **2.** National
  Academy **3.** National Army **4.** *IVR*
  Netherlands Antilles **5.** North America

Na   *Chem.* sodium

n/a   no account

NAA **1.** National Aeronautic Association
  (US) **2.** National Automobile Association
  (US)

NAACP   National Association for the
  Advancement of Colored Peoples (US)

NAAFI (naf′ē)   Navy, Army, and Air Force
  Institutes

NAB **1.** National Assistance Board
  2. National Association of Broadcasters

NABAC   National Association of Bank
  Auditors and Comptrollers

NAC   National Advisory Council

NACA   National Advisory Committee for
Aeronautics (now **NASA**)

NACODS   National Association of
Colliery Overmen, Deputies and Shotfirers

NAD   National Academy of Design (US)

Nah.   *Bib.* Nahum

NALGO (nal'gō)   National and Local
Government Officers' Association

NAM   National Association of
Manufacturers

NARE   National Association for Remedial
Education

NAS   **1.** National Academy of Sciences
2. National Association of Schoolmasters
3. Naval Air Station   **4.** Noise Abatement
Society   **5.** Nursing Auxiliary Service

NASA (nas'ǝ)   National Aeronautics and
Space Administration (US)

nat.   **1.** national   **2.** native   **3.** natural

NATKE   National Association of
Theatrical and Kine Employees

natl.   national

NATO (nā'tō)   North Atlantic Treaty
Organization

NATSOPA (nat sō'pǝ)   National Society
of Operative Printers and Assistants

naut.   nautical

nav.   **1.** naval   **2.** navigable
3. navigation   **4.** navy

NAVAR Combined Navigation and Radar System

navig. 1. navigation 2. navigator

NB 1. Brunswick 2. *nota bene* (*L.* note well)

Nb *Chem.* niobium

NBA 1. National Basketball Association 2. National Boxing Association

NBC National Broadcasting Corporation (US)

NBL National Book League

NBPI National Board for Prices and Incomes

NBS National Bureau of Standards (US)

NC 1. New Caledonia 2. nitrocellulose 3. no charge 4. North Carolina 5. Nurse Corps

NCAA National Collegiate Athletic Association (US)

NCB National Coal Board

NCCL National Council for Civil Liberties

nCi nanocurie

NCO Noncommissioned Officer

NCR 1. National Cash Register Company 2. no carbon required

NCTE National Council of Teachers of English

NCU National Cyclists' Union

ncv no commercial value

ND 1. no date 2. North Dakota

Nd *Chem.* neodymium
NDAC National Defense Advisory Commission (US)
NDPS National Data Processing Service
NE 1. Naval Engineer 2. New England 3. northeast
Ne *Chem.* neon
NEA 1. National Editorial Association 2. National Education Association 3. Newspaper Enterprise Association
NEB *New English Bible*
Neb., Nebr. Nebraska
NEC National Executive Committee
nec not elsewhere classified
NED *New English Dictionary*
NEDC National Economic Development Council
neg. negative(ly)
Neh. *Bib.* Nehemiah
nem. con. *nemine contradicente* (*L.* no one opposing)
nem. diss. *nemine dissentiente* (*L.* no one dissenting)
NEP New Economic Policy
NEPRA (nep′rə) National Egg Producers' Retail Association
NERC Natural Environment Research Council
nes not elsewhere specified
Neth. Netherlands

neurol. neurology
neut. 1. neuter 2. neutral
Nev. Nevada
NF 1. National Formulary (US)
2. Newfoundland 3. no funds
NFA National Farmers' Association
(Eire)
NFBTE National Federation of Building
Trades Employers
NFER National Foundation for
Educational Research
NFL National Football League (US)
Nfld. Newfoundland
NFS National Fire Service
NFT National Film Theatre
NFU National Farmers' Union
NFWI National Federation of Women's
Institutes
NG 1. National Guard 2. New Guinea
3. nitro-glycerine 4. no good
NGA National Graphical Association
NH New Hampshire
nH nanohenry
NHA National Housing Agency
NHBRC National House Builders'
Registration Council
NHI National Health Insurance
NHS National Health Service
NI 1. National Insurance 2. Naval
Intelligence 3. Northern Ireland

Ni *Chem.* nickel
NIA 1. National Intelligence Authority
2. Newspaper Institute of America
NIC 1. National Incomes Commission
2. *IVR* Nicaragua
NIG *IVR* Niger
NIH National Institutes of Health (US)
NIRA National Industrial Recovery Act
NIRC National Industrial Relations Court
NJ New Jersey
NL 1. National League 2. *IVR* Netherlands
n.l. 1. new line 2. *non licet* (*L.* it is not permitted) 3. *non liquet* (*L.* it is not clear)
NLC National Liberal Club
NLF National Liberation Front
NLRB National Labor Relations Board (US)
NLS National Library of Scotland
NM New Mexico
nm 1. nanometer 2. nautical mile 3. nonmetallic
NMI no middle initial
NMR nuclear magnetic resonance
NMU National Maritime Union
NNE north northeast
NNP Net National Product
NNW north northwest
No *Chem.* nobelium
No. 1. North(ern) 2. Number

n.o. *Cricket* not out
NOAA National Oceanic and Atmospheric Administration
nol. pros. *nolle prosequi* (*L.* do not continue)
nom. 1. nominal 2. nominative
noncom. noncommissioned
non obst. *non obstante* (*L.* notwithstanding)
non pros. *non prosequitur* (*L.* he does not prosecute)
non seq. *non sequitur* (*L.* it does not follow logically)
nop not otherwise provided for
Nor. 1. Norman 2. North 3. Norway 4. Norwegian
NORAD North American Air Defense Command
norm. normal
Northants. Northamptonshire
Northumb. Northumberland
nos. numbers
n.o.s. not otherwise specified
Notts. Nottinghamshire
Nov. November
nov. 1. novel 2. novice
NP 1. neuropsychiatric 2. *nisi prius* (*L.* unless previously judged) 3. Notary Public 4. noun phrase
Np *Chem.* neptunium

n.p. new paragraph
NPA Newspaper Publishers' Association
NPC National People's Congress
NPFA National Playing Fields Association
NPT normal pressure and temperature
NPU National Pharmaceutical Union
NR North Riding
nr. near
NRA 1. National Recovery Administration (US) 2. National Rifle Association
NRC Nuclear Research Council
NS 1. Nova Scotia 2. Nuclear Ship 3. Numismatic Society
ns nanosecond
n.s. 1. new series 2. new style 3. not specified 4. not sufficient
NSA 1. National Shipping Authority 2. National Standards Association 3. National Student Association
NSB National Savings Bank
NSC 1. National Safety Council 2. National Security Council (US)
NSF National Science Foundation (US)
n.s.f. not sufficient funds
NSMM National Society of Metal Mechanics
NSPCC National Society for the Prevention of Cruelty to Children

NSTIC Naval Scientific and Technical
Information Centre
NSU *Med.* non-specific urethritis
NSW New South Wales
NSY New Scotland Yard
NT 1. National Trust 2. New Testament
3. Northern Territory (Aust.)
4. Northwest Territories (Can.)
NTDA National Trade Development
Association
NTS National Trust for Scotland
NUAAW National Union of Agricultural
and Allied Workers
NUBE National Union of Bank Employees
NUDBTW National Union of Dyers,
Bleachers and Textile Workers
NUFLAT National Union of Footwear,
Leather and Allied Trades
NUGMW National Union of General and
Municipal Workers
NUHKW National Union of Hosiery and
Knitwear Workers
NUI National University of Ireland
NUIW National Union of Insurance
Workers
NUJ National Union of Journalists
NUL National Urban League
NUM National Union of Mineworkers
Num. *Bib.* Numbers
num. 1. number 2. numeral

numis. numismatics
NUPE (nyōō′pē) National Union of Public Employees
NUR National Union of Railwaymen
NUS 1. National Union of Seamen
2. National Union of Students
NUSMWCHDE National Union of Sheet Metal Workers, Coppersmiths, Heating and Domestic Engineers
NUT National Union of Teachers
NUTGW National Union of Tailors and Garment Workers
NV New Version (of the Bible)
n.v.d. no value declared
NW northwest
nW nanowatt
NWC National Water Council
NWP Northwest Provinces
NWT Northwest Territories (Can.)
NY New York
NYA National Youth Administration
NYC New York City
NYSE New York Stock Exchange
NZ *IVR* New Zealand
NZBS New Zealand Broadcasting Service
NZIC New Zealand Institute of Chemistry
NZIE New Zealand Institution of Engineers
NZIM New Zealand Institute of Management

NZLA New Zealand Library Association
NZSA New Zealand Statistical Association
NZSI New Zealand Standards Institute
NZVA New Zealand Veterinary Association

O

O 1. Ocean 2. octavo 3. October 4. Ohio 5. Old 6. Ontario 7. Oregon 8. *Chem.* oxygen
o/a on account of
O & M Organization and Methods
OAO Orbiting Astronomical Observatory
OAP Old Age Pension(er)
OAS 1. on active service 2. Organization of American States
OAU Organization of African Unity
OB 1. obstetrics 2. Old Bailey 3. Old Boy 4. outside broadcast
ob. 1. *obiit* (*L.* he/she died) 2. *obiter* (*L.* incidentally) 3. oboe
Obad. *Bib.* Obadiah
obb. *Mus.* obbligato (*It.* obligatory)
obdt. obedient

OBE   Officer of the Order of the British Empire

obj.   1. object 2. objection 3. objective

obl.   1. obligation 2. oblique 3. oblong

obs.   1. obscure 2. observation 3. observatory 4. obsolete

obstet.   obstetrics

obv.   obverse

OC   1. Observer Corps 2. Officer Commanding 3. Old Catholic 4. original cover

oc.   ocean

o.c.   *opere citato* (*L.* in the work cited)

o/c   overcharge

OCarm   Order of Carmelites

OCart   Order of Carthusians

occas.   occasional(ly)

occn.   occasion

OCD   Office of Civil Defense (US)

OCDM   Office of Civil and Defense Mobilisation (US)

oceanog.   oceanography

OCF   Officiating Chaplain to the Forces

OCR   *DP* Optical Character Reader

Oct.   October

oct.   1. octave 2. octavo

OCTU   Officer Cadets' Training Unit

OD   1. Doctor of Optometry 2. *oculus dexter* (*L.* right eye) 3. Officer of the Day

4. on demand 5. ordnance datum
6. outside diameter 7. overdraft
ODT Office of Defense Transportation
(US)
OE Old English
o.e. omissions excepted
OECD Organization for Economic
Cooperation and Development
OED *Oxford English Dictionary*
OEO Office of Economic Opportunity
(US)
OES Order of the Eastern Star
OF Old French
o.f. oil fired
off. 1. offer 2. office 3. officer
4. official
OFM Order of Friars Minor (Franciscans)
OFS Orange Free State
OG 1. Officer of the Guard 2. *Philately*
original gum
OGM Ordinary General Meeting
OGO Orbiting Geophysical Observatory
o.h.c. overhead camshaft
OHG Old High German
OHMS On His *or* Her Majesty's Service
o.h.v. overhead valve
OIRT International Organization of Radio
and Television
OIT Office of International Trade
Okla. Oklahoma

OL 1. *oculus laevus* (*L.* left eye) 2. Old Latin

OM Order of Merit

ONC Ordinary National Certificate

OND Ordinary National Diploma

ONI Office of Naval Intelligence

o.n.o. or near offer

Ont. Ontario

OOD Officer of the Day

OOG Officer of the Guard

OP 1. observation post 2. *Ordinis Praedicatorum* (*L.* Order of Preachers)

op. 1. opera 2. operation 3. operator 4. opposite 5. optical 6. opus

o.p. 1. out of print 2. overprint 3. overproof

OPA Office of Price Administration (US)

op. cit. *opere citato* (*L.* in the work cited)

OPEC (ō′pek) Organization of Petroleum Exporting Countries

ophthal. ophthalmology

opp. 1. opposed 2. opposite

opt. 1. optative 2. optical 3. optician 4. optics 5. optimum 6. optional

OR 1. Official Receiver 2. operational research 3. other ranks

o.r. owner's risk

ORC Officers' Reserve Corps

orch. orchestra(l)

ord.   **1.** ordained   **2.** order   **3.** ordinal   **4.** ordinance   **5.** ordinary   **6.** ordnance

Ore.   Oregon

org.   **1.** organic   **2.** organization   **3.** organized

orig.   **1.** origin   **2.** original   **3.** originally

ornith.   ornithology

Orth.   Orthodox

orth.   **1.** orthography   **2.** orthopaedic

OS   **1.** Old Saxon   **2.** Old School   **3.** Old Style   **4.** Ordinary Seaman   **5.** Ordnance Survey   **6.** Outsize

Os   *Chem.* osmium

o.s.   **1.** old series   **2.** only son   **3.** out of stock   **4.** outstanding

OSA   Order of Saint Augustine

OSB   Order of Saint Benedict

OSD   Order of Saint Dominic

OSF   Order of Saint Francis

OSP   Order of Saint Paul

OSRD   Office of Scientific Research and Development (US)

OSS   Office of Strategic Services (US)

OStJ   Officer of the Order of Saint John of Jerusalem

OT   **1.** occupational therapy   **2.** Old Testament   **3.** overtime

OTC   Officers' Training Corps (now **CCF**)

OU   **1.** Open University   **2.** Oxford University

OUP Oxford University Press
Ox., Oxf. Oxford (shire)
OXFAM (oks'fam) Oxford Committee for Famine Relief
Oxon. *Oxoniensis* (*L*. of Oxford)
oz. ounce
ozs. ounces
oz.t. ounce troy

P

P 1. Pastor 2. Pawn 3. petite 4. pitcher 5. *Chem.* phosphorus 6. police 7. *IVR* Portugal 8. post 9. power 10. President 11. pressure 12. Priest 13. Prince 14. prisoner 15. Probate 16. Protestant

p. 1. page 2. paragraph 3. part 4. participle 5. past 6. pawn 7. penny 8. per 9. peseta 10. peso 11. pint 12. pipe 13. pole 14. population 15. *post* (*L*. after) 16. power 17. pressure 18. *pro* (*L*. in favour of) 19. purl

PA 1. *IVR* Panama 2. Passenger Agent 3. Personal Assistant 4. Post Adjutant 5. Power of Attorney 6. Press Agent

7. Press Association **8.** Private Account
9. Public Address **10.** Publicity Agent
11. Publishers' Association
12. Purchasing Agent
P/A Private Account
Pa **1.** *Phys.* pascal **2.** *Chem.*
protactinium
Pa. Pennsylvania
p.a. **1.** participial adjective **2.** per annum
PABA *Chem.* para-aminobenzoic acid
PABX private automatic branch exchange
PAC (pak) Political Action Committee
Pac. Pacific
PACE (pās) *DP* Precision Analog
Computing Equipment
PAK *IVR* Pakistan
Pak. Pakistan
Pal. Palestine
paleont. paleontology
pam. pamphlet
PAN *Chem.* peroxyacetyl nitrate
Pan. Panama
pan. **1.** panchromatic **2.** panoramic
P & L Profit and Loss
P & O Peninsular and Oriental Steamship
Company
p & p postage and packing
par. **1.** paragraph **2.** parallel
3. paraphrase **4.** parenthesis **5.** parish
6. parochial

Para. Paraguay(an)
paren. parenthesis
Parl. Parliament(ary)
Parl. proc. Parliamentary procedure
part. 1. participial 2. participle
3. particular 4. partner
partn. partnership
pass. 1. passage 2. passenger
3. *passim* (*L.* here and there) 4. passive
pat. 1. patent 2. patented
patd. patented
path., pathol. 1. pathological
2. pathology
Pat. Off. Patent Office
pat. pend. patent pending
patt. pattern
PAU Pan American Union
Pav. Pavilion
PAX private automatic exchange
PAYE Pay As You Earn
payt. payment
PB 1. Pharmacopoeia Britannica
2. *Philosophiae Baccalaureus* (*L.* Bachelor
of Philosophy) 3. Prayer Book
4. Premium Bond
Pb *Chem.* lead
PBA Public Buildings Administration
(US)
PBS Public Broadcasting System (US)
PBT President of the Board of Trade

PBX private branch exchange
PC 1. Panama Canal 2. Parish Council
  3. Parish Councillor 4. Past Commander
  5. Pioneer Corps 6. Police Constable
  7. Post Commander 8. Press Council
  9. Prince Consort 10. Privy Council
  11. Privy Councillor
pc. 1. piece 2. price
p.c. 1. per cent 2. postcard 3. *post
cibum* (*L.* after meals)
p/c 1. petty cash 2. price current
PCC Provincial Congress Committee
PCM *DP* 1. pulse code modulation
  2. punched card machine
PCS Principal Clerk of Session
pct. percent
PCV positive crankcase ventilation
PD 1. *per diem* (*L.* by the day)
  2. *Pharmaciae Doctor* (*L.* Doctor of
  Pharmacy) 3. *Philosophiae Doctor* (*L.*
  Doctor of Philosophy) 4. Police
  Department 5. postal district
Pd. *Chem.* palladium
pd. 1. paid 2. passed
p.d. *Elec.* potential difference
PDB *Chem.* paradichlorobenzene
PdB *Pedagogiae Baccalaureus* (*L.*
  Bachelor of Pedagogy) (US)
PdD *Pedagogiae Doctor* (*L.* Doctor of
  Pedagogy) (US)

PdM *Pedagogiae Magister* (*L.* Master of Pedagogy) (US)
PDSA People's Dispensary for Sick Animals
PDT Pacific Daylight Time (US)
PE 1. *IVR* Peru 2. physical education 3. potential energy 4. Presiding Elder 5. printer's error 6. Professional Engineer 7. Protestant Episcopal
p/e price/earnings
PeB *Pediatriae Baccalaureus* (*L.* Bachelor of Pediatrics)
p.e.c. photoelectric cell
ped. 1. pedal 2. pedestal
PEI Prince Edward Island
Pemb. Pembrokeshire (former county)
PEN (pen) International Association of Poets, Playwrights, Editors, Essayists and Novelists
pen. 1. peninsula 2. penitentiary
Penn. Pennsylvania
Pent. 1. *Bib.* Pentateuch 2. Pentecost
pent. pentagon
PEP Political and Economic Planning
Per. 1. Persia 2. Persian
per. 1. period 2. person
PERA Production Engineering Research Association
perf. 1. perfect 2. perforated 3. performance

perf. part.   perfect participle
perm.   **1.** permanent **2.** permission
perp.   **1.** perpendicular **2.** perpetual
per pro.   *per procurationem* (*L.* on behalf of)
Pers.   **1.** Persia **2.** Persian
pers.   **1.** person **2.** personal
PERT (pŭrt)   *DP* Program Evaluation and Review Technique
pert.   pertaining
Pet.   *Bib.* Peter
petrog.   petrography
petrol.   petrology
PF   Procurator Fiscal
pf   **1.** perfect **2.** pfennig **3.** pianoforte **4.** preferred **5.** proof
p.f.   *Mus. più forte* (*It.* a little louder)
PFA   Professional Footballers' Assocation
PFC   Private First Class (US)
pfd.   preferred
pfg.   pfennig
PG   **1.** paying guest **2.** Postgraduate **3.** Procurator General
Pg.   **1.** Portugal **2.** Portuguese
pg.   page
PGA   Professional Golfers' Association
PGM   Past Grand Master
PH   Purple Heart
ph.   phase
PHA   Public Housing Administration (US)

phar. 1. pharmaceutical 2. pharmacist 3. pharmacology 4. pharmacopoeia 5. pharmacy

PharB *Pharmaciae Baccalaureus* (*L.* Bachelor of Pharmacy)

PharD *Pharmaciae Doctor* (*L.* Doctor of Pharmacy)

PharM *Pharmaciae Magister* (*L.* Master of Pharmacy)

pharm. 1. pharmaceutical 2. pharmacist 3. pharmacology 4. pharmacopoeia 5. pharmacy

pharmacol. pharmacology

PhB *Philosophiae Baccalaureus* (*L.* Bachelor of Philosophy)

PhC Pharmaceutical Chemist (US)

PhD *Philosophiae Doctor* (*L.* Doctor of Philosophy)

PhG Graduate in Pharmacy (US)

Phil. 1. Philadelphia 2. Philharmonic 3. *Bib.* Philippians 4. Philippine

phil. 1. philology 2. philosopher 3. philosophical 4. philosophy

Philem. *Bib.* Philemon

philol. 1. philological 2. philology

philos. 1. philosopher 2. philosophical 3. philosophy

phon. 1. phonetics 2. phonology

phonet. phonetics

phonol. phonology

phot. **1.** photograph **2.** photographic
3. photography
photom. photometry
phr. **1.** phrase **2.** phraseology
phren. phrenology
PHS Public Health Service (US)
phys. **1.** physical **2.** physician
3. physics **4.** physiological **5.** physiology
phys. ed. physical education
physiol. **1.** physiological **2.** physiology
PI *IVR* Philippine Islands
PIB Petroleum Information Bureau
PIO Public Information Office
pizz. *Mus. pizzicato* (*It.* plucking strings
with fingers)
PJ **1.** Police Justice **2.** Presiding Justice
3. Probate Judge
PK psychokinesis
pk. **1.** pack **2.** park **3.** peak **4.** peck
pkg. **1.** package **2.** packing
pkt. **1.** packet **2.** pocket
PKU *Med.* phenylketonuria
pkwy. parkway
PL **1.** Poet Laureate **2.** *IVR* Poland
3. Public Library
P/L Profit and Loss
Pl. Place
pl. **1.** place **2.** plate **3.** platoon
4. plural
PLA Port of London Authority

plat. 1. plateau 2. platoon
PLO Palestine Liberation Organization
PLP Parliamentary Labour Party
PLR Public Lending Right
plupf. pluperfect
plur. 1. plural 2. plurality
PM 1. Past Master 2. Paymaster
3. Police Magistrate 4. Postmaster
5. *post meridiem* (*L.* after noon) 6. Post
Mortem 7. Prime Minister 8. Provost
Marshal
Pm *Chem.* promethium
pm. premium
p.m. 1. phase modulation 2. *post
meridiem*
PMA Production and Marketing
Administration (US)
PMG 1. Paymaster General
2. Postmaster General 3. Provost Marshal
General
PMO Principal Medical Officer
Pmr. Paymaster
PMRAFNS Princess Mary's Royal Air
Force Nursing Service
PMT pre-menstrual tension
PMX private manual exchange
p.n. promissory note
PNdb perceived noise decibel
PNEU Parents' National Education Union
PO 1. Patent Office 2. Personnel Officer

3. Petty Officer **4.** Pilot Officer **5.** Postal Order **6.** Post Office **7.** Province of Ontario

Po *Chem.* polonium

POA Prison Officers' Association

POB Post Office Box

POD **1.** pay on delivery **2.** Post Office Department

POE **1.** Port of Embarkation **2.** Port of Entry

poet. **1.** poetic **2.** poetical **3.** poetry

POEU Post Office Engineering Union

POGO (pō'gō) Polar Orbiting Geophysical Observatory

POL Petroleum, Oil and Lubricants

Pol. **1.** Poland **2.** Polish

pol. **1.** political **2.** politics

polio. poliomyelitis

polit. **1.** political **2.** politics

poly. polytechnic

POO Post Office Order

POP Post Office preferred

pop. **1.** popular **2.** popularly **3.** population

Port. **1.** Portugal **2.** Portuguese

POS point of sale

pos. **1.** position **2.** positive **3.** possessive

POSB Post Office Savings Bank (now NSB)

poss. **1.** possession **2.** possessive
3. possible **4.** possibly

pot. potential

POUNC Post Office Users' National
Council

POW **1.** Prince of Wales **2.** prisoner of
war

POWU Post Office Workers' Union

PP **1.** Parish Priest **2.** Past President

pp **1.** *per procurationem* (*L.* on behalf of)
2. *Mus.* pianissimo (*It.* very soft)

pp. pages

p.p. **1.** parcel post **2.** past participle
3. postpaid **4.** *post prandium* (*L.* after
meals) **5.** prepaid

ppd. **1.** postpaid **2.** prepaid

PPE Philosophy, Politics, and Economics

pph. pamphlet

ppm parts per million

PPRA Past President of the Royal
Academy

PPS **1.** Parliamentary Private Secretary
2. *post postscriptum* (*L.* additional
postscript)

PQ Province of Quebec

p.q. previous question

PR **1.** Proportional Representation
2. Public Relations **3.** Puerto Rico

Pr *Chem.* praseodymium

Pr. **1.** Priest **2.** Prince **3.** Provençal

pr. 1. pair 2. paper 3. power
4. preferred 5. present 6. price
7. pronoun

PRA President of the Royal Academy

PRB Pre-Raphaelite Brotherhood

PRC People's Republic of China

PRCA President of the Royal Cambrian Academy

PRCP President of the Royal College of Physicians

PRCS President of the Royal College of Surgeons

Preb. Prebendary

prec. preceding

pred. predicate

pref. 1. preface 2. prefatory
3. preference 4. preferred 5. prefix

prefab. prefabricated

prelim. preliminary

prem. premium

prep. 1. preparation 2. preparatory
3. preposition

Pres. 1. Presbyterian 2. President

pres. 1. present 2. presidency
3. presidential

Presb. Presbyterian

pres. part. present participle

pret. preterite

prev. 1. previous 2. previously

PRIA President of the Royal Irish Academy

PRIBA President of the Royal Institute of British Architects

prim. 1. primary 2. primitive

prin. 1. principal 2. principally 3. principle

priv. 1. private 2. privative

PRO 1. Public Records Office 2. Public Relations Officer

pro. 1. professional 2. prostitute (also pro)

prob. 1. probable 2. probably 3. problem

proc. 1. procedure 2. proceedings 3. process 4. proclamation

prod. 1. produce 2. produced 3. product

Prof. Professor

prof. profession

prog. 1. programme 2. progress 3. progressive

PROI President of the Royal Institute of Oil Painters

prom. 1. promenade 2. promontory

pron. 1. pronominal 2. pronoun 3. pronounced 4. pronunciation

prop. 1. proper 2. properly 3. property 4. proposition 5. proprietor

Propr. Proprietor

pros. prosody
Pros. Atty. Prosecuting Attorney
Prot. 1. Protectorate 2. Protestant
Prov. 1. Provençal 2. *Bib.* Proverbs
3. Province
prov. 1. proverb 2. proverbial
3. province 4. provincial 5. provisional
prox. *proximo* (*L.* next month)
PRS President of the Royal Society
prs. pairs
PRSA President of the Royal Scottish
Academy
PRSE President of the Royal Society of
Edinburgh
Prus. 1. Prussia 2. Prussian
PS 1. Paddle Steamer 2. Parliamentary
Secretary 3. Passenger Steamer
4. permanent secretary 5. Pharmaceutical
Society 6. Philological Society
7. Philosophical Society 8. phrase
structure 9. Physical Society
10. Physiological Society 11. Police
Sergeant 12. postscript 13. Private
Secretary 14. Privy Seal 15. prompt
side 16. Public School
Ps. *Bib.* Psalms
PSA President of the Society of
Antiquaries
pseud. pseudonym
psf pounds per square foot

PSI   **1.** Pharmaceutical Society of Ireland
  2. Public Services International
psi   pounds per square inch
psso   *Knitting* pass slipped stitch over
PST   Pacific Standard Time (US)
PSV   Public Service Vehicle
psych.   **1.** psychological **2.** psychology
psychoanal.   psychoanalysis
psychol.   **1.** psychological **2.** psychology
PT   **1.** Pacific Time **2.** physical therapy
  3. physical training **4.** Postal Telegraph
  5. Pupil Teacher **6.** Purchase Tax
Pt   *Chem.* platinum
pt.   **1.** part **2.** patient **3.** payment
  4. pint **5.** point **6.** port **7.** preterite
p.t.   **1.** past tense **2.** *pro tempore* (*L.* for
  the time being)
PTA   **1.** Parent-Teacher Association
  2. Passenger Transport Authority
pta.   peseta
Pte.   Private
ptg.   printing
PTO   please turn over
pts.   **1.** parts **2.** payments **3.** pints
  4. points **5.** ports
PTU   Plumbing Trades Union
PTV   Public Television
Pty.   Proprietary
Pu   *Chem.* plutonium

pub. **1.** public **2.** publication
3. published **4.** publisher **5.** publishing
publ. **1.** publication **2.** published
3. publisher
pur. purchase
PUWP Polish United Workers' Party
PVC polyvinyl chloride
Pvt., Pvte. Private
PW **1.** Policewoman **2.** prisoner of war
PWA Public Works Administration (US)
PWD Public Works Department
PWP Polish Workers' Party
pwt. pennyweight
PX **1.** post exchange (US) **2.** private
exchange
PY *IVR* Paraguay

Q

Q **1.** Quarto **2.** Quebec **3.** Queen
4. Question
q. **1.** *quadrans* (*L.* farthing) **2.** quart
3. quarter **4.** quarterly **5.** quarto
6. quasi **7.** queen **8.** query **9.** question
10. quetzal **11.** quintal **12.** quire
QAB Queen Anne's Bounty

QARANC Queen Alexandra's Royal Army Nursing Corps

QARNNS Queen Alexandra's Royal Naval Nursing Service

QB 1. Queen's Bench 2. Queen's Bishop

QBP Queen's Bishop's Pawn

QC 1. Quartermaster Corps 2. Queen's Counsel

QDG Queen's Dragoon Guards

q.e. *quod est* (*L.* which is)

QED *quod erat demonstrandum* (*L.* which was to be proved)

QEF *quod erat faciendum* (*L.* which was to be done)

QEI *quod erat inveniendum* (*L.* which was to be found)

QF quick firing

QFSM Queen's Fire Service Medal

QHC Queen's Honorary Chaplain

QHDS Queen's Honorary Dental Surgeon

QHNS Queen's Honorary Nursing Sister

QHP Queen's Honorary Physician

QHS Queen's Honorary Surgeon

q.i.d. *quater in die* (*L.* four times daily)

QIDN Queen's Institute of District Nursing

QKt Queen's Knight

QKtP Queen's Knight's Pawn

ql. quintal

q.l. *quantum libet* (*L.* as much as you please)

Qld. Queensland

qlty. quality

QM 1. Quartermaster 2. Queen's Messenger

q.m. *quaque mane* (*L.* every morning)

QMC Quartermaster Corps

QMG Quartermaster General

QMS Quartermaster Sergeant

QN Queen's Knight

Qn. Queen

qn. 1. question 2. quotation

q.n. *quaque nocte* (*L.* every night)

QNP Queen's Knight's Pawn

qnty. quantity

QOCH Queen's Own Cameron Highlanders

QOH Queen's Own Hussars

QP Queen's Pawn

q.p. *quantum placet* (*L.* as much as you please)

QPM Queen's Police Medal

QPR Queen's Park Rangers

qq. 1. quartos 2. questions

QR Queen's Rook

qr. 1. *quadrans* (*L.* farthing) 2. quarter 3. quarterly 4. quire

QRIH Queen's Royal Irish Hussars

QRP Queen's Rook's Pawn

QRR   Queen's Royal Rifles

QS   Quarter Sessions

q.s.   **1.** *quantum sufficit* (*L.* a sufficient quantity) **2.** quarter section

QSO   quasi-stellar object

qt.   **1.** quantity **2.** quart

q.t.   quiet

qto.   quarto

qtr.   **1.** quarter **2.** quarterly

qty.   quantity

qu.   **1.** quart **2.** quarter **3.** quarterly **4.** queen **5.** query **6.** question

quad.   **1.** quadrangle **2.** quadrant **3.** quadrilateral **4.** quadruplicate

qual.   **1.** qualified **2.** quality

Quango (kwaŋ′gō)   quasi autonomous non-governmental organization

quar.   **1.** quarter **2.** quarterly

Que.   Quebec

ques.   question

quor.   quorum

quot.   quotation

q.v.   *quod vide* (*L.* which see)

qy.   query

R

R 1. Rabbi 2. *Chem.* radical
3. Rankine 4. Réaumur 5. Rector
6. *Regina* (*L.* Queen) 7. Republican
8. *Phys.* resistance 9. *Eccles.* response
10. *Rex* (*L.* King) 11. *Phys.* roentgen
12. Rook 13. *IVR* Rumania

r. 1. radius 2. railway 3. range 4. rare
5. received 6. *recipe* (*L.* take) 7. rector
8. redactor 9. residence 10. resides
11. retired 12. right 13. rises 14. river
15. road 16. rod 17. royal 18. rubber
19. ruble 20. rules 21. runs 22. rupee

RA 1. *IVR* Argentina 2. Ratepayers'
Association 3. Rear Admiral 4. Regular
Army (US) 5. *Astronomy* right ascension
6. Royal Academician 7. Royal Academy
8. Royal Arch 9. Royal Artillery

Ra *Chem.* radium

RAA 1. Royal Academy of Arts 2. Royal
Australian Artillery

RAAF Royal Australian Air Force

RAC 1. Royal Aero Club 2. Royal Arch
Chapter 3. Royal Armoured Corps
4. Royal Automobile Club

RACA Royal Automobile Club of
Australia

rall.

RACI   Royal Australian Chemical Insitute
RACP   Royal Australian College of Physicians
RACS   Royal Australian College of Surgeons
RAD   Royal Academy of Dancing
rad   radian
rad.   1. radical 2. radius 3. *radix* (*L.* root)
RADA (rä′də)   Royal Academy of Dramatic Art
RADC   Royal Army Dental Corps
RAdm   Rear Admiral
RAE   Royal Aircraft Establishment
RAEC   Royal Army Educational Corps
RAes   Royal Aeronautical Society
RAF   Royal Air Force
RAFVR   Royal Air Force Volunteer Reserve
RAGC   Royal and Ancient Golf Club, St Andrews
RAI   1. Royal Anthropological Institute 2. Royal Archaeological Institute
RAIA   Royal Australian Institute of Architects
RAIC   Royal Architectural Institute of Canada
rall.   *Mus. rallentando* (*It.* gradually slackening speed)

RAM 1. Royal Academy of Music
2. Royal Arch Mason
RAMC Royal Army Medical Corps
RAN Royal Australian Navy
R & B *Mus.* rhythm and blues
R & D research and development
R & R rest and recuperation
RAOC Royal Army Ordnance Corps
RAPC Royal Army Pay Corps
RAS 1. Royal Aeronautical Society
2. Royal Agricultural Society 3. Royal
Asiatic Society 4. Royal Astronomical
Society
RASC Royal Army Service Corps (now
RCT)
RAVC Royal Army Veterinary Corps
RAX rural automatic exchange
RB 1. *IVR* Botswana 2. Rifle Brigade
Rb *Chem.* rubidium
RBA Royal Society of British Artists
RBE relative biological effectiveness
RBL Royal British Legion
RBS Royal Society of British Sculptors
RC 1. *IVR* China 2. Red Cross
3. Reformed Church 4. reinforced
concrete 5. Reserve Corps 6. Roman
Catholic 7. Royal College
RCA 1. *IVR* Central African Republic
2. Radio Corporation of America 3. Royal
College of Art

RCAA **1.** Royal Cambrian Academy of Art **2.** Royal Canadian Academy of Arts
RCAF Royal Canadian Air Force
RCamA Royal Cambrian Academy of Art
RCB *IVR* Congo
RCCh Roman Catholic Church
rcd. received
RCGP Royal College of General Practitioners
RCH *IVR* Republic of Chile
RCI Royal Canadian Institute
RCM Royal College of Music
RCMP Royal Canadian Mounted Police
RCN **1.** Royal Canadian Navy **2.** Royal College of Nursing
RCO Royal College of Organists
RCOG Royal College of Obstetricians and Gynaecologists
RCP **1.** Royal College of Physicians **2.** Royal College of Preceptors
rcpt. receipt
RCS **1.** Royal College of Science **2.** Royal College of Surgeons **3.** Royal Corps of Signals
RCSI Royal College of Surgeons in Ireland
RCT Royal Corps of Transport
Rct. Recruit
RCVS Royal College of Veterinary Surgeons

RD **1.** Royal Naval Reserve Decoration
2. rural delivery
R/D Refer to Drawer
Rd. Road
rd. **1.** rendered **2.** road **3.** round
RDC Rural District Council
RDE Research and Development
Establishment
RDF Royal Dublin Fusiliers
RDI Royal Designer for Industry
RDS Royal Dublin Society
RdTh *Chem.* radiothorium
RE **1.** *Chem.* rare-earth elements **2.** Real
Estate (US) **3.** Reformed Episcopal
4. Right Excellent **5.** Royal Engineers
6. Royal Exchange **7.** Royal Society of
Etchers and Engravers
Re *Chem.* rhenium
re. rupee
REA Rural Electrification Administration
(US)
rec. **1.** receipt **2.** recipe **3.** record
4. recorded **5.** recorder **6.** recording
recd. received
recit. *Mus. recitativo* (*It.* recitative)
REconS Royal Economic Society
Rect. **1.** Rector **2.** Rectory
rect. **1.** receipt **2.** rectangle
red. **1.** reduce **2.** reduced

redupl.   **1.** reduplicate **2.** reduplication **3.** reduplicative

ref.   **1.** referee **2.** reference **3.** referred **4.** reformation **5.** reformed **6.** reformer **7.** refund

Ref. Ch.   Reformed Church

refl.   **1.** reflection **2.** reflective **3.** reflex **4.** reflexive

Reg.   **1.** Regent **2.** Regiment **3.** *Regina* (*L.* Queen)

reg.   **1.** regent **2.** regiment **3.** region **4.** register **5.** registered **6.** registrar **7.** registry **8.** regular **9.** regularly **10.** regulation **11.** regulator

regd.   registered

Reg. Prof.   Regius Professor

Regt.   **1.** Regent **2.** Regiment

rel.   **1.** relating **2.** relative **3.** relatively **4.** released **5.** religion **6.** religious

relig.   **1.** religion **2.** religious

REM   **1.** rapid eye movement **2.** Roentgen equivalent in man

REME (rĕ″mē)   Royal Electrical and Mechanical Engineers

Renf.   Renfrewshire (former county)

Rep.   **1.** Repertory **2.** Representative **3.** Republic **4.** Republican

rep.   **1.** repeat **2.** report **3.** reported **4.** reporter **5.** representative **6.** reprint

repr. 1. represented 2. representing
  3. reprint 4. reprinted
repro. reproduction
rept. 1. receipt 2. report
Repub. 1. Republic 2. Republican
req. 1. request 2. required
  3. requisition
RES 1. Royal Economic Society 2. Royal
  Entomological Society
res. 1. research 2. reserve 3. residence
  4. resides 5. residue 6. resigned
  7. resistance 8. resolution
resp. 1. respective 2. respectively
  3. respiration 4. respondent
restr. restaurant
ret. 1. retain 2. retired 3. return
  4. returned
Rev. 1. *Bib.* Revelation 2. Reverend
rev. 1. revenue 2. reverse 3. review
  4. reviewed 5. revise 6. revised
  7. revision 8. revolution 9. revolving
Revd. Reverend
RF 1. radio frequency 2. rapid fire
  3. Royal Fusiliers 4. Rugby Football
Rf *Mus. rinforzando* (*It.* reinforcing)
RFA Royal Field Artillery
RFC Rugby Football Club
RFD rural free delivery (US)
RFL Rugby Football League
RFU Rugby Football Union

rgd.   registered

RGG   Royal Grenadier Guards

RGN   Registered General Nurse

RGO   Royal Greenwich Observatory

RGS   Royal Geographical Society

RGSA   Royal Geographical Society of Australasia

Rgt.   Regiment

RH   1. *IVR* Republic of Haiti 2. Royal Highness

Rh   1. rhesus 2. *Chem.* rhodium

r.h.   1. relative humidity 2. right hand

RHA   1. Royal Hibernian Academy 2. Royal Horse Artillery

r.h.d.   right hand drive

rheo.   *Elec.* rheostat

rhet.   1. rhetoric 2. rhetorical

RHF   Royal Highland Fusiliers

RHG   Royal Horse Guards

RHistS   Royal Historical Society

RHS   1. Royal Historical Society 2. Royal Horticultural Society 3. Royal Humane Society

RI   1. *Regina et Imperatrix* (*L.* Queen and Empress) 2. *IVR* Republic of Indonesia 3. *Rex et Imperator* (*L.* King and Emperor) 4. Rhode Island 5. Royal Institute of Painters in Water Colours 6. Royal Institution

RIA   Royal Irish Academy

RIAC Royal Irish Automobile Club
RIAI Royal Institute of the Architects of Ireland
RIAM Royal Irish Academy of Music
RIAS Royal Incorporation of Architects in Scotland
RIBA Royal Institute of British Architects
RIC 1. Royal Institute of Chemistry
2. Royal Irish Constabulary
RICS Royal Institution of Chartered Surveyors
RIF Royal Irish Fusiliers
RIGB Royal Institution of Great Britain
RIIA Royal Institute of International Affairs
RIM *IVR* Republic of Mauritania
RINA Royal Institution of Naval Architects
RIOP Royal Institute of Oil Painters
RIP *requiescat in pace* (*L.* may he/she rest in peace)
RIPA Royal Institution of Public Administration
RIPHH Royal Institute of Public Health and Hygiene
rit. *Mus. ritardando* (*It.* decrease pace)
riv. river
RJ road junction
RJA Royal Jersey Artillery
RJLI Royal Jersey Light Infantry

RJM   Royal Jersey Militia
RL   **1.** *IVR* Republic of Lebanon **2.** Rugby League
RLSS   Royal Life Saving Society
rly.   railway
RM   **1.** *IVR* Malagasy Republic **2.** reichsmark **3.** Resident Magistrate **4.** Royal Mail **5.** Royal Marines
rm.   **1.** ream **2.** room
RMA   **1.** Royal Marine Artillery **2.** Royal Military Academy
RMCC   Royal Military College of Canada
RMCS   Royal Military College of Science
RMetS   Royal Meteorological Society
RMM   *IVR* Republic of Mali
RMO   Resident Medical Officer
RMP   Royal Military Police
RMS   **1.** Railway Mail Service **2.** Royal Mail Service **3.** Royal Mail Steamer **4.** Royal Medical Society **5.** Royal Meteorological Society **6.** Royal Microscopical Society
rms   *Math.* root mean square
RN   **1.** Registered Nurse **2.** Royal Navy
Rn   *Chem.* radon
RNA   ribonucleic acid
RNAS   Royal Naval Air Service (now FAA)
rnd.   round

RNIB   Royal National Institute for the Blind
RNID   Royal National Institute for the Deaf
RNLI   Royal National Lifeboat Institution
RNR   1. Royal Naval Reserve   2. *IVR* Zambia
RNS   Royal Numismatic Society
RNVR   Royal Naval Volunteer Reserve
RNZAF   Royal New Zealand Air Force
RNZN   Royal New Zealand Navy
RO   1. Receiving Officer   2. Regimental Order   3. Registered Office   4. Royal Observatory
ro.   1. recto   2. roan   3. rood
ROC   Royal Observer Corps
ROI   Royal Institute of Oil Painters
ROK   *IVR* Republic of Korea
Rom.   1. Roman   2. Romance   3. Romania   4. Romanian   5. Romanic   6. *Bib.* Romans
rom.   roman (type)
Rom. Cath.   Roman Catholic
RoSPA (ros'pə)   Royal Society for the Prevention of Accidents
rot.   1. rotating   2. rotation
ROTC   Reserve Officers' Training Corps (US)
RP   1. Received Pronunciation   2. Reformed Presbyterian   3. Regius

Professor **4.** retinitis pigmentosa (tunnel vision) **5.** Royal Society of Portrait Painters

RPC   Royal Pioneer Corps

RPD   *Rerum Politicarum Doctor* (*L.* Doctor of Political Science)

rph   revolutions per hour

RPhilS   **1.** Royal Philatelic Society **2.** Royal Philharmonic Society

rpm   **1.** resale price maintenance **2.** revolutions per minute

RPO   Railway Post Office

RPS   **1.** Royal Philatelic Society **2.** Royal Philharmonic Society **3.** Royal Photographic Society

rps   revolutions per second

rpt.   **1.** repeat **2.** report

RQ   respiratory quotient

RR   **1.** Right Reverend **2.** Rolls Royce

RRA   Royal Regiment of Artillery

RRC   Royal Red Cross

RRE   Radar Research Establishment

RRF   Royal Regiment of Fusiliers

RRP   Recommended Retail Price

RS   **1.** Revised Statutes **2.** Royal Scots **3.** Royal Society

Rs.   rupees

r.s.   right side

RSA   **1.** Royal Scottish Academy **2.** Royal Society of Antiquaries **3.** Royal

Society of Arts **4.** Royal Society of
Australia
RSAC Royal Scottish Automobile Club
RSAI Royal Society of Antiquaries of
Ireland
RSAM Royal Scottish Academy of Music
RSC **1.** Royal Shakespeare Company
2. Royal Society of Canada
RSD Royal Society of Dublin
RSE Royal Society of Edinburgh
RSF Royal Scots Fusiliers
RSFSR Russian Soviet Federated
Socialist Republic
RSG **1.** Regional Seats of Government
2. Royal Scots Greys
RSGB Radio Society of Great Britain
RSGS Royal Scottish Geographical
Society
RSH Royal Society for the Promotion of
Health
RSigs Royal Corps of Signals
RSL Royal Society of Literature
RSM **1.** Regimental Sergeant-Major
2. Royal School of Music **3.** Royal Society
of Medicine **4.** *IVR* San Marino
RSNZ Royal Society of New Zealand
RSO **1.** Railway Sorting Office
2. Railway Sub-Office **3.** Resident
Surgical Officer

RSPB Royal Society for the Protection of Birds

RSPCA Royal Society for the Prevention of Cruelty to Animals

RSPCC Royal Scottish Society for the Prevention of Cruelty to Children

RSR *IVR* Rhodesia

RSS 1. *Regiae Societatis Socius* (*L.* Fellow of the Royal Society) 2. Royal Statistical Society

RSSA Royal Scottish Society of Arts

RSV Revised Standard Version (of the Bible)

RSVP *répondez s'il vous plaît* (*Fr.* please reply)

RSW Royal Scottish Society of Painters in Water Colours

RT 1. radio telegraphy 2. radio telephony

rt. right

rte. route

Rt. Hon. Right Honourable

RTI Round Table International

RTO Railway Transport Officer

RTPI Royal Town Planning Institute

RTR Royal Tank Regiment

Rt. Rev. Right Reverend

RTS Religious Tract Society

RU 1. *IVR* Burundi 2. Readers' Union 3. Rugby Union

Ru *Chem.* ruthenium
RUA Royal Ulster Academy
RUAS Royal Ulster Agricultural Society
RUC Royal Uster Constabulary
RUR Royal Ulster Rifles
Russ. 1. Russia 2. Russian
RV Revised Version (of the Bible)
RVC 1. Rifle Volunteer Corps 2. Royal Veterinary College
RVCI Royal Veterinary College of Ireland
RVIA Royal Victoria Institute of Architects (Aust.)
RVO Royal Victorian Order
RW 1. Right Worshipful 2. Right Worthy 3. Royal Warrant
RWA *IVR* Rwanda
RWS Royal Society of Painters in Water Colours
rwy., ry. railway
RYA Royal Yachting Association
RYS Royal Yacht Squadron
RYT reference your telegram *or* telex
RZS Royal Zoological Society
RZSI Royal Zoological Society of Ireland
RZSS Royal Zoological Society of Scotland

S

S **1.** Sabbath **2.** Saint **3.** Saturday
4. Saxon **5.** School **6.** Seaman
7. Senate **8.** September **9.** *Signor*
10. Society **11.** South **12.** Southern
13. *Chem.* sulphur **14.** Sunday **15.** *IVR*
Sweden
s second
s. **1.** section **2.** see **3.** semi- **4.** series
5. shilling **6.** sign **7.** signed **8.** silver
9. singular **10.** sire **11.** son
12. soprano **13.** steamer **14.** substantive
SA **1.** Salvation Army **2.** Seaman
Apprentice **3.** Society of Antiquaries
4. Society of Arts **5.** Society of Authors
6. South Africa **7.** South America
8. South Australia
Sa *Chem.* samarium (Obs.)
s.a. **1.** *secundum artem* (*L.* according to
art) **2.** semi-annual **3.** *sine anno* (*L.*
undated)
SAA **1.** Small Arms Ammunition
2. South African Airways **3.** Standards
Association of Australia
SAAF South African Air Force
Sab. Sabbath

SABC   South African Broadcasting
Corporation
SAC   **1.** Scottish Automobile Club
2. Senior Aircraftman **3.** Strategic Air
Command (US)
SACTU   South African Congress of Trade
Unions
SACW   Senior Aircraftwoman
SADC   Scottish Agricultural Development
Council
SAE   **1.** Society of Aeronautical
Engineers **2.** Society of Automotive
Engineers (US)
s.a.e.   stamped addressed envelope
SAfr.   **1.** South Africa **2.** South African
SAIF   South African Industrial Federation
SALA   South African Library Association
SALP   South African Labour Party
SALT (sôlt)   Strategic Arms Limitation
Talks
SAM   surface-to-air missile
SAm.   **1.** South America **2.** South
American
Sam.   *Bib.* Samuel
SANS   South African Naval Service
Sans., Sansk.   Sanskrit
SANU   Sudan African National Union
SANZ   Standards Association of New
Zealand
SAP   South African Police

SAPA South African Press Association
SAR **1.** Sons of the American Revolution
2. South African Republic
Sar. **1.** Sardinia **2.** Sardinian
SARAH (sāər'ə) Search and Rescue and
Homing
SAS **1.** Scandinavian Airlines System
2. *Societatis Antiquariorum Socius* (*L.*
Fellow of the Society of Antiquaries)
Sask. Saskatchewan
SAT South Australian Time
Sat. **1.** Saturday **2.** Saturn
SATB *Mus.* soprano, alto, tenor, bass
SAVS Scottish Anti-Vivisection Society
Sax. **1.** Saxon **2.** Saxony
sax. saxophone
SAYE Save As You Earn
SB **1.** *Scientiae Baccalaureus* (*L.*
Bachelor of Science) **2.** Special Branch
3. Statute Book
Sb *Chem.* antimony
sb. substantive
SBA Small Business Administration (US)
SBIC Small Business Investment
Corporation (US)
SBN Standard Book Number
SC **1.** Sanitary Corps **2.** Security Council
(of the UN) **3.** Signal Corps **4.** South
Carolina **5.** Special Constable **6.** Staff
College **7.** Staff Corps **8.** Supreme Court

Sc *Chem.* scandium

Sc. 1. Scots 2. Scottish

sc. 1. scale 2. scene 3. science
4. *scilicet* (*L.* namely) 5. screw
6. scruple 7. *sculpsit* (*L.* he/she engraved it)

s.c. 1. small capitals 2. supercalendared

Scand. 1. Scandinavia 2. Scandinavian

SCAP Supreme Command Allied Powers

SCAT supersonic commercial air transport

ScB *Scientiae Baccalaureus* (*L.* Bachelor of Science)

SCCE Scottish Central Committee on English

ScD *Scientiae Doctor* (*L.* Doctor of Science)

SCDA Scottish Community Drama Association

SCE Scottish Certificate of Education

SCF 1. Save the Children Fund 2. Senior Chaplain to the Forces

sch. 1. scholar 2. school 3. schooner

sci. 1. science 2. scientific

SCL Student of Civil Law

SCLC Southern Christian Leadership Conference (US)

SCM 1. State Certified Midwife
2. Student Christian Movement

ScM *Scientiae Magister* (*L.* Master of Science)

Scot. **1.** Scotland **2.** Scottish

SCR Senior Common Room

scr. scruple

Script. **1.** Scriptural **2.** Scripture

sculp. **1.** *sculpsit* (*L.* he/she engraved it) **2.** sculptor **3.** sculptress **4.** sculpture **5.** sculptural

SCWS Scottish Cooperative Wholesale Society

SD **1.** Senior Deacon **2.** South Dakota **3.** *IVR* Swaziland

S/D sight draft

sd. sound

s.d. **1.** *sine die* (*L.* without date) **2.** standard deviation

SDC single data converter

SDD Scottish Development Department

SDF Social Democratic Federation

SDLP Social and Democratic Labour Party (N. Ireland)

SDP Social Democratic Party

SDR special drawing right (from **IMF**)

SDS Students for a Democratic Society (US)

SE **1.** Society of Engineers **2.** southeast **3.** Stock Exchange

Se *Chem.* selenium

SEAC South-East Asia Command

SEATO (sē′tō) Southeast Asia Treaty Organization

SEC Securities and Exchange Commission (US)

sec. 1. secant 2. second 3. secondary 4. secretary 5. section 6. security

sech *Math.* hyperbolic secant

sec. leg. *secundum legum* (*L.* according to law)

sec. reg. *secundum regulam* (*L.* according to rule)

sect. section

Secy. Secretary

sed. 1. sediment 2. sedimentation

sel. 1. selected 2. selection

Selk. Selkirkshire (former county)

Sem. 1. Seminary 2. Semitic

sem. 1. semester (US) 2. semi-colon

SEN State Enrolled Nurse

Sen. 1. Senate 2. Senator 3. Senior

Sep. 1. September 2. Septuagint

sep. 1. sepal 2. separate

Sept. 1. September 2. Septuagint

seq. 1. sequel 2. *sequens* (*L.* the following)

ser. 1. serial 2. series 3. sermon

Serb. 1. Serbia 2. Serbian

Serg. Sergeant

serv. 1. servant 2. service

Sess. Session

SET   Selective Employment Tax
SF   **1.** *IVR* Finland   **2.** San Francisco
  3. Science Fiction   **4.** Signal Frequency
  5. Sinn Fein   **6.** Society of Friends
sf.   *Mus.* sforzando (*It.* giving a strong
accent on a single note or chord)
SFA   **1.** Scottish Football Association
  2. Sweet Fanny Adams, ie nothing at all
SFC   Sergeant First Class
SG   **1.** Scots Guards   **2.** Solicitor General
  3. Surgeon General (US)
s.g.   **1.** senior grade   **2.** specific gravity
SGA   Society of Graphic Arts
SGB   Scottish Gas Board
sgd.   signed
SGP   *IVR* Singapore
Sgt.   Sergeant
Sgt. Maj.   Sergeant Major
sh.   **1.** share   **2.** sheep   **3.** sheet
  4. shilling
SHA   sidereal hour angle
SHAEF (shāf)   Supreme Headquarters
Allied Expeditionary Forces
Shak.   Shakespeare
SHAPE (shāp)   Supreme Headquarters
Allied Powers Europe
SHF   superhigh frequency
s.h.m.   simple harmonic motion
SHO   *Med.* Senior House Officer
shp   shaft horsepower

shpt. shipment
shr. share
shtg. shortage
SI 1. Order of the Star of India
2. *Système Internationale* (international metric system)
Si *Chem.* silicon
Sib. 1. Siberia 2. Siberian
Sic. 1. Sicilian 2. Sicily
SICA Society of Industrial and Cost Accountants of Canada
SIDS sudden infant death syndrome
SIE Society of Industrial Engineers
Sig. 1. *Signor* 2. *Signore*
sig. 1. signal 2. signature 3. *signor*
sing. singular
sinh *Math.* hyperbolic sine
SIS Secret Intelligence Service
SJ 1. Society of Jesus (Jesuits)
2. Solicitors' Journal
s.j. *sub judice* (*L.* under consideration)
SJC Supreme Judicial Court
SJD *Scientiae Juridicae Doctor* (*L.* Doctor of Juridical Science)
sk. sack
SKC Scottish Kennel CLub
Skt. Sanskrit
SL 1. Sergeant-at-Law 2. Solicitor at Law 3. Squadron Leader

s.l.   *sine loco* (*L.* without place of publication)

SLA   Scottish Library Association

SLADE (slād)   Society of Lithographic Artists, Designers, Engravers and Process Workers

Slav.   **1.** Slavic **2.** Slavonic

SLBM   submarine-launched ballistic missile

sld.   **1.** sailed **2.** sealed

SLP   Socialist Labour Party

s.l.p.   *sine legitima prole* (*L.* without lawful issue)

SM   **1.** *Sceintiae Magister* (*L.* Master of Science) **2.** Sergeant Major **3.** Soldier's Medal **4.** State Militia (US)

Sm   *Chem.* samarium

SMA   Surplus Marketing Administration

SME   *IVR* Surinam

Smith. Inst.   Smithsonian Institute (US)

SMLondSoc   *Societatis Medicae Londiniensis Socius* (*L.* Member of the London Medical Society)

SMM   *Sancta Mater Maria* (*L.* Holy Mother Mary)

SMMB   Scottish Milk Marketing Board

SMO   Senior Medical Officer

SMOM   Sovereign and Military Order of Malta

s.m.p. *sine mascula prole* (*L.* without male issue)

SN *IVR* Senegal

Sn *Chem.* tin

s.n. *secundum naturam* (*L.* according to nature)

SNAP systems for nuclear auxiliary power

SNCF *Société Nationale des Chemins de Fer Français* (*Fr.* French National Railways)

SNIWB Scottish National Institute for War-Blinded

SNO **1.** Scottish National Orchestra **2.** Senior Naval Officer

SNP Scottish National Party

Snr. Senior

SO **1.** Scottish Office **2.** Signal Officer **3.** Special Order **4.** Staff Officer **5.** Stationery Office

s.o. **1.** seller's option **2.** shipping order

SOAS School of Oriental and African Studies

SOB son of a bitch (US Slang)

Soc. **1.** Socialist **2.** Society

sociol. **1.** sociological **2.** sociology

S of S *Bib.* Song of Songs

S of Sol. *Bib.* Song of Solomon

SOGAT (sō'gat) Society of Graphical and Allied Trades

Sol. **1.** Solicitor **2.** Solomon
sol. **1.** soluble **2.** solution
Som. Somerset
SONAR (sō′när) Sound Navigation and Ranging
SOP standard operating procedure
sop. soprano
SOR sale or return
SOS Save Our Souls
SP **1.** Shore Patrol **2.** Socialist Party **3.** starting price **4.** Submarine Patrol
Sp. **1.** Spain **2.** Spaniard **3.** Spanish
sp. **1.** special **2.** species **3.** specific **4.** specimen **5.** spelling **6.** spirit **7.** sport
s.p. *sine prole* (*L.* without issue)
SPAB Society for the Protection of Ancient Buildings
Span. **1.** Spaniard **2.** Spanish
SPCK Society for Promoting Christian Knowledge
spec **1.** special **2.** specification **3.** speculation
specif. **1.** specific **2.** specifically **3.** specification
sp. gr. specific gravity
sp. ht. specific heat
SPOE Society of Post Office Executives
SPQR **1.** *Senatus Populusque Romanus* (*L.* the Senate and people of Rome) **2.** small profits, quick return

SPR   Society for Psychical Research

SPRC   Society for the Prevention and Relief of Cancer

s.p.s.   *sine prole superstite* (*L.* without surviving issue)

spt.   seaport

sp. vol.   specific volume

Sq.   1. Squadron 2. Square

sq.   1. sequence 2. *sequens* (*L.* the following) 3. squadron 4. square

sq. ft.   square foot

sq. in.   square inch

SR   1. self-raising (flour) 2. Society of Radiographers

Sr   *Chem.* strontium

Sr.   1. Senhor 2. Senior 3. Señor 4. Sister

Sra.   1. Senhora 2. Señora

SRBM   short range ballistic missile

SRC   1. Science Research Council 2. Student Representative Council

SRI   *Sacrum Romanum Imperium* (*L.* Holy Roman Empire)

SRN   State Registered Nurse

SRO   1. standing room only 2. Statutory Rules and Orders

SRS   *Societatis Regiae Socius* (*L.* Fellow of the Royal Society)

Srta.   1. Senhorita 2. Señorita

SRU   Scottish Rugby Union

SS 1. *Sancti* (*L.* Saints) 2. *scilicet* (*L.* namely) 3. Secretary of State 4. Social Security 5. steamship 6. Sunday School 7. supersonic 8. *supra scriptum* (*L.* written above)

SSA Social Security Administration (US)

SSAFA Soldiers', Sailors' and Airmen's Families Association

SSB Social Security Board (US)

SSC Solicitor to the Supreme Court

SSD *Sacrae Scripturae Doctor* (*L.* Doctor of Sacred Scripture)

SS.D. *Sanctissimus Dominus* (*L.* Most Holy Lord, ie the Pope)

SSE south southeast

SSgt. Staff Sergeant

SSHA Scottish Special Housing Association

SSM surface-to-surface missile

SSPCA Scottish Society for the Prevention of Cruelty to Animals

SSR Soviet Socialist Republic

SSRC Social Science Research Council

SSS 1. Secretary of State for Scotland 2. selective service system (US)

SST supersonic transport

SSTA Scottish Secondary Teachers' Association

SSW south southwest

St. 1. Saint 2. Strait 3. Street

st. **1.** stanza **2.** statute **3.** stet
 4. stitch **5.** stone **6.** strait **7.** street
 8. stumped

s.t. short ton

Sta. **1.** Santa **2.** Station

sta. **1.** stationary **2.** stator

Staffs. Staffordshire

STB *Sacrae Theologiae Baccalaureus* (*L.*
 Bachelor of Sacred Theology)

STC short-title catalogue

STD **1.** *Sacrae Theologiae Doctor* (*L.*
 Doctor of Sacred Theology) **2.** sexually
 transmitted disease **3.** subscriber trunk
 dialling

std. standard

STE Society of Telecommunications
 Engineers

Ste. *Sainte* (*Fr.* female saint)

ster. sterling

stge. storage

Stir. Stirlingshire (former county)

stk. stock

STL *Sacrae Theologiae Licentiatus* (*L.*
 Licentiate of Sacred Theology)

STM *Sacrae Theologiae Magister* (*L.*
 Master of Sacred Theology)

STOL (stōl, stol) short take-off and
 landing

STP **1.** *Sanctae Theologiae Professor* (*L.*

Professor of Sacred Theology) **2.** standard temperature and pressure

str. **1.** steamer **2.** straight **3.** strait **4.** string

stratig. stratigraphy

STS Scottish Text Society

Sts. Saints

STUC Scottish Trades Union Congress

STV Scottish Television

SU **1.** strontium unit **2.** *IVR* Union of Soviet Socialist Republics

sub. **1.** subaltern **2.** subeditor **3.** subject **4.** submarine **5.** subscription **6.** substitute **7.** suburb **8.** suburban **9.** subway

SUBAW Scottish Union of Bakers and Allied Workers

subj. **1.** subject **2.** subjective **3.** subjectively **4.** subjunctive

subst. **1.** substantive **2.** substitute

Suff. **1.** Suffolk **2.** Suffragan

suff. **1.** sufficient **2.** suffix

SUM surface-to-underwater missile

Sun. Sunday

sup. **1.** superior **2.** superlative **3.** supine **4.** supplement **5.** supplementary **6.** supply **7.** *supra* (*L.* above)

super. **1.** superfine **2.** superior

supp., suppl. 1. supplement
2. supplementary
supr. 1. superior 2. supreme
Supt. Superintendent
surg. 1. surgeon 2. surgery 3. surgical
surv. 1. survey 2. surveying
3. surveyor
SV *Sancta Virgo* (*L.* Holy Virgin)
s.v. *sub verbo* or *sub voce* (*L.* under a
specified word)
SW 1. short wave 2. southwest
Sw. 1. Sweden 2. Swedish 3. Swiss
SWA *IVR* South West Africa
Swed. 1. Sweden 2. Swedish
SWG standard wire gauge
Swit., Switz. Switzerland
SWAPO (swä'pō) South West Africa
People's Organization
Sx. Sussex
SY 1. *IVR* Seychelles 2. steam yacht
SYHA Scottish Youth Hostels
Association
syll. 1. syllable 2. syllabus
sym. 1. symbol 2. symmetrical
3. symphony 4. symptom
syn. 1. synonym 2. synonymous
3. synonymy
SYP Society of Young Publishers
SYR *IVR* Syria

Syr.   **1.** Syria **2.** Syriac **3.** Syrian
syst.   system

T

T   **1.** tablespoon **2.** tablespoonful
  3. technician **4.** temperature
  5. territory **6.** *Phys.* tesla **7.** Testament
  8. *IVR* Thailand **9.** time **10.** town
  11. township **12.** *Chem.* tritium
  13. Tuesday
t   tonne
t.   **1.** tare **2.** target **3.** teaspoon
  4. teaspoonful **5.** telephone
  6. temperature **7.** tempo **8.** *tempore* (*L.*
  in the time of) **9.** tenor **10.** tense
  11. time **12.** tome **13.** *tomus* (*L.*
  volume) **14.** ton **15.** town
  16. township **17.** transit **18.** transitive
  19. troy
TA   **1.** Teaching Assistant (US)
  2. Territorial Army **3.** transactional
  analysis
Ta   *Chem.* tantalum
TAB   **1.** Totalizator Agency Board
  (Aust.) **2.** typhoid, paratyphoid A and
  paratyphoid B vaccine

tab. 278

tab. 1. table 2. tablet 3. tabulation
TAC 1. Tactical Air Command 2. Trades Advisory Council
TAM Television Audience Measurement
tan *Math.* tangent
tanh *Math.* hyperbolic tangent
TANU Tanganyikan African National Union
Tas., Tasm. 1. Tasmania 2. Tasmanian
TAT *Psychol.* thematic apperception test
TAVR Territorial and Army Volunteer Reserve
TB 1. torpedo boat 2. Trial Balance 3. tubercle bacillus 4. tuberculosis
Tb *Chem.* terbium
t.b. trial balance
TBD torpedo-boat destroyer
tbl *Knitting* through back of loops
tbs. 1. tablespoon 2. tablespoonful
TC 1. Tank Corps 2. Tennis Club 3. Town Clerk 4. Town Councillor 5. Twin Carburettors
Tc *Chem.* technetium
tc. tierce
TCBM transcontinental ballistic missile
TCD Trinity College, Dublin
TCL Trinity College of Music, London
TD 1. Territorial Decoration 2. touchdown 3. Treasury Department
Te *Chem.* tellurium

tech. 1. technical 2. technology
technol. 1. technological 2. technology
tel. 1. telegram 2. telegraph
3. telegraphic 4. telephone
telecomm. telecommunications
teleg. 1. telegram 2. telegraph
3. telegraphic 4. telegraphy
temp. 1. temperate 2. temperature
3. temporary 4. *tempore* (*L.* in the time of)
ten. 1. tenor 2. *Mus.* tenuto (*It.* sustained)
Tenn. Tennessee
Ter. 1. Terrace 2. Territory
term. 1. terminal 2. termination
3. terminology
Terr. 1. Terrace 2. Territory
TES *Times Educational Supplement*
Test. Testament
Teut. 1. Teuton 2. Teutonic
Tex. 1. Texan 2. Texas
TF 1. Task Force 2. Territorial Force
TFR Territorial Force Reserve
TG *IVR* Togo
t.g. type genus
TGWU Transport and General Workers' Union
Th *Chem.* thorium
Th. Thursday

ThB *Theologiae Baccalaureus* (*L.* Bachelor of Theology)

ThD *Theologiae Doctor* (*L.* Doctor of Theology)

theat. theatrical

theol. 1. theologian 2. theological 3. theology

theor. theorem

theos. 1. theosophical 2. theosophy

therap. therapeutic

Thess. *Bib.* Thessalonians

THI temperature-humidity index

ThL Theological Licentiate

ThM *Theologiae Magister* (*L.* Master of Theology)

Thos. Thomas

Thurs. Thursday

THWM Trinity High Water Mark

TI 1. Technical Institute 2. Textile Institute

Ti *Chem.* titanium

t.i.d. *tres in die* (*L.* three times daily)

Tim. *Bib.* Timothy

tinct. tincture

TIR *Transports Internationaux Routiers* (*Fr.* International Road Transport)

TIROS (tīər′ōs) Television and Infrared Observation Satellite (US)

Tit. *Bib.* Titus

tit. title

tk. truck
TKO technical knockout
tkt. ticket
TL 1. total loss 2. trade list 3. truck load
Tl *Chem.* thallium
TLS *Times Literary Supplement*
TM transcendental meditation
Tm *Chem.* thulium
TMO telegraph money order
TN *IVR* Tunisia
tn. 1. ton 2. town 3. train
tng. training
TNT *Chem.* trinitrotoluene, a high explosive
TO 1. Telegraph Office 2. Transport Officer
t.o. turn over
Tob. *Bib.* Tobit
tog. together
topog. 1. topographical 2. topography
tot. total
tox. toxicology
TP Transvaal Province
tp. 1. township 2. troop
t.p. title page
TPI Town Planning Institute
tpk. turnpike
tpr. teleprinter
TR *IVR* Turkey

tr. 1. trace 2. transitive 3. translated 4. translation 5. translator 6. transpose 7. treasurer 8. trill 9. trustee

trad. traditional

trans. 1. transaction 2. transferred 3. transformer 4. transit 5. transitive 6. translated 7. translation 8. translator 9. transparent 10. transport 11. transportation 12. transpose 13. transverse

transf. transferred

transl. 1. translated 2. translation 3. translator

transp. 1. transparent 2. transport

trav. 1. traveller 2. travels

TRE Telecommunications Research Establishment

Treas. 1. Treasurer 2. Treasury

t.r.f. tuned radio frequency

TRH Their Royal Highnesses

trig. 1. trigonometrical 2. trigometry

tripl. triplicate

trit. triturate

TRM trademark

trop. 1. tropic 2. tropical

trs. 1. transfer 2. transpose

TSB Trustee Savings Bank

TSH 1. Their Serene Highnesses 2. thyroid-stimulating hormone

tsp. 1. teaspoon 2. teaspoonful

u.

TSSA   Transport Salaried Staffs'
Association

TT   **1.** teetotal **2.** teetotaller **3.** Tourist
Trophy **4.** *IVR* Trinidad and Tobago
5. tuberculin tested

TU   Trade Union

Tu.   Tuesday

TUC   Trades Union Congress

Tues.   Tuesday

Turk.   **1.** Turkey **2.** Turkish

TV   television

TVA   Tennessee Valley Authority

TWA   Trans-World Airlines (US)

TWI   Training Within Industry

twp.   township

Ty.   Territory

typ., typog.   **1.** typographer
2. typographic **3.** typographical
4. typography

typw.   **1.** typewriter **2.** typewritten

U

U   **1.** Uncle **2.** Union **3.** United
4. Universal **5.** University **6.** *Chem.*
uranium **7.** *IVR* Uruguay

u.   **1.** uniform **2.** unit **3.** upper

UAC Ulster Automobile Club

UAE United Arab Emirates

UAM underwater-to-air missile

UAR United Arab Republic (now Arab Republic of Egypt)

UAW United Automobile Workers (US)

UC 1. University College 2. Urban Council

u.c. upper case

UCAR Union of Central African Republics

UCATT Union of Construction, Allied Trades and Technicians

UCCA (uk'ə) Universities Central Council on Admissions

UCP United Country Party (Aust.)

UDA Ulster Defence Association

UDC 1. Universal Decimal Classification 2. Urban District Council

UDI Unilateral Declaration of Independence

UDR Ulster Defence Regiment

UDT. United Dominions Trust

UEFA (yoō ā'fə) Union of European Football Associations

UF United Free Church of Scotland

UFO (yoō'ef ō', yoō'fō) unidentified flying object

UFT United Federation of Teachers

UFU Ulster Farmers' Union

UGC University Grants Committee

UHF ultrahigh frequency

UHT ultra heat treated

UK United Kingdom

UKAEA United Kingdom Atomic Energy
Authority

UKAPE United Kingdom Association of
Professional Engineers

UL 1. Underwriters' Laboratories (US)
2. University Library

ult. 1. ultimate 2. ultimately 3. *ultimo*
(*L.* last month)

UMIST University of Manchester
Institute of Science and Technology

UMWA United Mine Workers of America

UN United Nations

UNA United Nations Association

UNADA United Nations Atomic
Development Authority

UNAEC United Nations Atomic Energy
Commission

UNCIO United Nations Conference on
International Organization

UNCITRAL United Nations Commission
on International Trade Law

UNCP United Nations Conference of
Plenipotentiaries

UNCTAD United Nations Conference on
Trade and Development

UNDP United Nations Development
Programme

UNDRO United Nations Disaster Relief
Organization
UNEC United Nations Education
Conference
UNEDA United Nations Economic
Development Administration
UNEF United Nations Emergency Force
UNEP United Nations Environmental
Programme
UNESCO (yoo nes′kō) United Nations
Educational, Scientific, and Cultural
Organization
UNETAS United Nations Emergency
Technical Aid Service
UNFAO United Nations Food and
Agriculture Organization
UNFC United Nations Food Conference
UNGA United Nations General Assembly
UNHCR United Nations High
Commission for Refugees
UNIC United Nations Information Centre
UNICEF (yoo′nə sef′) United Nations
International Children's Emergency Fund
UNIDO (yoo′nə dō) United Nations
Industrial Development Organization
UNIO United Nations Information
Organization
Unit. Unitarian
UNITAR United Nations Institute for
Training and Research

Univ.   **1.** Universalist   **2.** University
univ.   **1.** universal   **2.** universally
  3. university
UNKRA   United Nations Korean Relief
  Administration
UNO (yōō′en ō′, yōō′nō)   United Nations
  Organization
UNPOC   United Nations Peace
  Observation Commission
UNRRA (un′rə)   United Nations Relief and
  Rehabilitation Administration
UNRWA   United Nations Relief and
  Works Agency
UNSF   United Nations Special Fund
UNTAA   United Nations Technical
  Assistance Administration
UNTT   United Nations Trust Territory
UP   **1.** United Presbyterian   **2.** United
  Press   **3.** United Provinces
UPA   United Printers' Association
UPI   United Press International (US)
UPL   International Institute for the
  Unification of Private Law
UPOW   Union of Post Office Workers
  (also **UPW**)
UPU   Universal Postal Union
UPW   Union of Post Office Workers (also
  UPOW)
URTU   United Road Transport Union
Uru.   Uruguay

US **1.** Under-Secretary **2.** United Services **3.** United States

u.s. **1.** *ubi supra* (*L.* where mentioned above) **2.** *ut supra* (*L.* as above)

USA **1.** Union of South Africa **2.** United States Army **3.** *IVR* United States of America

USAEC United States Atomic Energy Commission

USAF United States Air Force

USAFI United States Armed Forces Institute

USAID United States Agency for International Development

USAR United States Army Reserve

USCG United States Coast Guard

USCL United Society for Christian Literature

USCSC United States Civil Service Commission

USDA United States Department of Agriculture

USDAW (us′dô′) Union of Shop, Distributive and Allied Workers

USDC United States Department of Commerce

USDI United States Department of the Interior

USDL United States Department of Labor

USES United States Employment Service

USGPO   United States Government Printing Office

USGS   United States Geological Survey

USI   1. Union of Students in Ireland
2. United Schools International

USIA   United States Information Agency

USM   1. underwater-to-surface missade
2. United States Mail 3. United States Marines 4. United States Mint

USMA   United States Military Academy

USMC   1. United States Marine Corps
2. United States Maritime Commission

USN   United States Navy

USNA   1. United States National Army
2. United States Naval Academy

USNG   United States National Guard

USNR   United States Naval Reserve

USO   United Service Organizations (US)

USP   United States Pharmacopoeia

USPG   United Society for the Propagation of the Gospel

USPHS   United States Public Health Service

USPO   United States Post Office

USR   United States Reserves

USRC   United States Reserve Corps

USS   1. United States Senate 2. United States Service 3. United States Ship
4. Universities Superannuation Scheme

USSCt   United States Supreme Court

USSR   Union of Soviet Socialist Republics
usu.   usually
USW   **1.** ultrashort waves **2.** ultrasonic waves
UT   Universal Time
Ut.   Utah
ut dict.   *ut dictum* (*L.* as directed)
ut sup.   *ut supra* (*L.* as above)
UU   Ulster Unionist
UV   ultraviolet
UWT   Union of Women Teachers
ux.   *uxor* (*L.* wife)

V

V   **1.** *Roman numeral for* 5 **2.** *Chem.* vanadium **3.** *IVR* Vatican City **4.** *Math.* vector **5.** velocity **6.** Venerable **7.** Vicar **8.** Vice **9.** victory **10.** Viscount **11.** volt
v   velocity
v.   **1.** vacuum **2.** valley **3.** valve **4.** ventral **5.** verb **6.** verse **7.** version **8.** *verso* (*L.* left-hand page) **9.** *versus* (*L.* against) **10.** very **11.** *vice* (*L.* in the place of) **12.** *vide* (*L.* see) **13.** village **14.** violin **15.** vise **16.** vocative

17. voice **18.** volt **19.** voltage
20. volume
VA **1.** Royal Order of Victoria and Albert
2. Veterans' Administration (US) **3.** Vicar
Apostolic **4.** Vice Admiral
Va. Virginia
vac. **1.** vacancy **2.** vacant **3.** vacuum
VAD Voluntary Aid Detachment
val. **1.** valuation **2.** value
VAR visual-aural range
var. **1.** variant **2.** variation **3.** variety
4. variometer **5.** various
VAT Value Added Tax
Vat. Vatican
v.aux. verb auxiliary
vb. **1.** verb **2.** verbal
VC **1.** Vatican City **2.** Veterinary Corps
(US) **3.** Vice-Chairman
4. Vice-Chancellor **5.** Vice-Consul
6. Victoria Cross **7.** Viet Cong
VD **1.** venereal disease **2.** Royal Naval
Volunteer Reserve Decoration (now **VRD**)
v.d. **1.** vapour density **2.** various dates
VDC Volunteer Defence Corps
VDU *DP* visual display unit
VE Victory in Europe
veg. **1.** vegetable **2.** vegetarian
3. vegetation
vel. **1.** vellum **2.** velocity

Ven. 1. Venerable 2. Venezuela 3. Venice 4. Venus
Ver. 1. Vermont 2. Version
ver. 1. verse 2. version
VERA (vēər'ə) 1. versatile experimental reactor assembly 2. vision electronic recording apparatus
vers *Math.* versed sine
vert. vertical
vet. 1. veteran 2. veterinarian 3. veterinary
VF 1. video frequency 2. voice frequency
VFR visual flight rules
VFW Veterans of Foreign Wars (US)
VG Vicar-General
v.g. very good
VHF very high frequency
VI Virgin Islands
v.i. 1. verb intransitive 2. *vide infra* (*L.* see below)
Vic. Victoria
vic. 1. vicar 2. vicarage 3. vicinity
vil. village
v.imp. verb impersonal
VIP very important person
Vis. Viscount
viz. *videlicit* (*L.* namely)
v.l. *varia lectio* (*L.* variant reading)
VLF very low frequency
VM Victoria Medal

VMAI   Veterinary Medical Association of Ireland

VMD   *Veterinariae Medicinae Doctor* (*L.* Doctor of Veterinary Medicine)

VMH   Victoria Medal of Honour

VN   *IVR* Vietnam

v.n.   verb neuter

VO   1. Royal Victorian Order 2. very old

vo.   *verso* (*L.* left-hand page)

voc.   1. vocal 2. vocalist 3. vocation 4. vocative

vocab.   vocabulary

vol.   1. volatile 2. volcano 3. volume 4. volunteer

VOLAR (vō′lär)   Volunteer Army

vols.   volumes

VP   Vice-President

v.p.   1. vapour pressure 2. verb passive

VR   *Victoria Regina* (*L.* Queen Victoria)

v.r.   verb reflexive

VRD   Royal Navy Volunteer Reserve Decoration

V.Rev.   Very Reverend

VRI   *Victoria Regina Imperatrix* (*L.* Victoria Queen and Empress)

VS   Veterinary Surgeon

vs.   *versus* (*L.* against)

v.s.   *vide supra* (*L.* see above)

VSA   Voice Stress Analyser

VSO 1. very superior old 2. Voluntary Service Overseas
VSOP very superior old pale
vss. versions
VT variable time
Vt. Vermont
v.t. verb transitive
Vte. *Vicomte* (*Fr.* Viscount)
VTOL vertical take-off and landing
VTR video tape recorder
VU volume unit
vul., vulg. vulgar
Vulg. Vulgate
vv. 1. verses 2. violins 3. volumes
v.v. 1. *vice versa* (*L.* interchanged) 2. *viva voce* (*L.* spoken aloud)
VW Very Worshipful
vy. very

W

W 1. *Chem.* tungsten 2. Wales 3. Washington 4. *Phys.* watt 5. Wednesday 6. Welsh 7. west 8. western 9. women's
w. 1. waist 2. warden 3. warehouse 4. week 5. weight 6. white 7. wide

8. width **9.** wife **10.** with **11.** won
12. work **13.** wrong
WA **1.** West Africa **2.** Western Australia
WAAA Women's Amateur Athletic
Association
WAAC (wak) Women's Auxiliary Army
Corps (now **WRAC**)
WAAF (waf) Women's Auxiliary Air
Force (Now **WRAF**)
WAC (wak) Women's Army Corps (US)
WAF (waf) Women in the Air Force (US)
w.a.f. with all faults
WAG *IVR* Gambia
WAL *IVR* Sierra Leone
WAN *IVR* Nigeria
War. Warwickshire
Wash. Washington
WASP (wosp) White Anglo-Saxon
Protestant (US)
WAVES (wāvz) Women Appointed for
Voluntary Emergency Service (US)
W/B waybill
Wb *Phys.* weber
w.b. **1.** water ballast **2.** westbound
WBA World Boxing Association
WBC World Boxing Council
WC West Central
w.c. **1.** water closet **2.** without charge
WCC World Council of Churches
W/Cdr. Wing Commander

WCTU   Women's Christian Temperance Union
WD   1. *IVR* Dominica 2. War Department 3. Works Department
wd.   1. ward 2. word 3. would
WEA   Workers' Educational Association
WEC   World Energy Conference
Wed.   Wednesday
w.e.f.   with effect from
WEU   Western European Union
w.f.   *Ptg.* wrong fount
WFA   White Fish Authority
WFTU   World Federation of Trade Unions
WG   1. *IVR* Grenada 2. Welsh Guards
w.g.   wire gauge
WGA   Writers' Guild of America
Wg. Cdr.   Wing Commander
WHO (hōō)   World Health Organization
Wh   watt-hour
WI   1. West Indian 2. West Indies 3. Windward Islands 4. Women's Institute
Wilts.   Wiltshire
WIPO   World Intellectual Property Organization
Wis.   Wisconsin
wk.   1. week 2. work
wkly.   weekly
WL   1. *IVR* St Lucia 2. water line 3. wavelength

WLA   Women's Land Army
WLF   Women's Liberal Federation
WMA   World Medical Association
wmk.   watermark
WMO   World Meteorological Association
WNP   Welsh Nationalist Party
WNW   west northwest
WO   1. War Office 2. Warrant Officer
3. wait order
w/o   without
WOC   without compensation
Worcs.   Worcestershire (former county)
WP   1. weather permitting 2. without
prejudice
WPC   1. Woman Police Constable
2. World Petroleum Congress 3. World
Power Conference (now **WEC**)
WPI   World Press Institute
wpm   words per minute
WR   West Riding, Yorkshire
WRAAC   Women's Royal Australian
Army Corps
WRAAF   Women's Royal Australian Air
Force
WRAC (rak)   Women's Royal Army Corps
WRAF (raf)   Women's Royal Air Force
WRANS   Women's Royal Australian
Naval Service
WRE   Weapons Research Establishment
(Aust.)

WRI 298

WRI   Women's Rural Institute
WRNR   Women's Royal Naval Reserve
WRNS (renz)   Women's Royal Naval
Service
wrnt.   warrant
WRVS   Women's Royal Voluntary
Service
WS   1. *IVR* Western Samoa   2. West
Saxon   3. Writer to the Signet
WSW   west southwest
wt.   weight
WV   *IVR* St Vincent
W.Va.   West Virginia
WVS   Women's Voluntary Service (now
WRVS)
WWI   World War 1
WWII   World War 2
WWF   World Wildlife Fund
WWW   World Weather Watch
WX   women's extra large size
Wy., Wyo.   Wyoming
WZO   World Zionist Organization

X

X **1.** Christ **2.** Christian **3.** Cross
4. *Cin.* for adult audiences only **5.** *Roman numeral for* 10

x. extra

x.d. *Fin.* ex dividend

Xe *Chem.* xenon

x.i. *Fin.* ex interest

XL extra large

Xm., Xmas Christmas

Xn. Christian

Xnty. Christianity

XQ cross question

x.r. *Fin.* ex rights

x.ref. cross reference

xs. expenses

Xt. Christ

Xty. Christianity

x.w. *Fin.* ex warrants

Y

Y *Chem.* yttrium
y. 1. yard 2. year
YB Year Book
Yb *Chem.* ytterbium
YC 1. Young Conservative 2. Youth Club
yd. yard
yeo. yeoman(ry)
YFC Young Farmers' Club
YHA Youth Hostels Association
YLI Yorkshire Light Infantry
YMCA Young Men's Christian Association
YMHA Young Men's Hebrew Association
YOP Youth Opportunities Commission (of MSC)
Yorks. Yorkshire
yr. 1. year 2. younger 3. your
yrs. 1. years 2. yours
YS Young Socialists
YT Yukon Territory
YU *IVR* Yugoslavia
Yugo. Yugoslavia
YV *IVR* Venezuela
YWCA Young Women's Christian Association
YWHA Young Women's Hebrew Association

Z

Z **1.** *Chem.* atomic number **2.** *Elec.* impedance **3.** *IVR* Zambia **4.** *Astronomy* zenith distance

z. **1.** zero **2.** zone

ZA *IVR* South Africa

ZADC Zinc Alloy Die Casters' Association

ZANU (zän′o͞o) Zimbabwe African National Union

ZAPU (zäp′o͞o) Zimbabwe African People's Union

ZC Zionist Congress

ZD zenith distance

Zech. *Bib.* Zechariah

Zeph. *Bib.* Zephaniah

ZF zero frequency

Zn *Chem.* zinc

ZOA Zionist Organization of America

Zod. Zodiac

zoochem. zoochemistry

zoogeog. zoogeography

zool. **1.** zoological **2.** zoology

ZPG zero population growth

ZR *IVR* Zaire

Zr *Chem.* zirconium

ZS Zoological Society

ZST Zone Standard Time

SIGNS & SYMBOLS

ASTRONOMY

Astronomical Bodies

☉ 1. The Sun 2. Sunday
☾ ☽ 1. The Moon 2. Monday
● New Moon
☽ ☾ First Quarter
○ Full Moon
☾ ☾ Last Quarter
☿ 1. Mercury 2. Wednesday
♀ 1. Venus 2. Friday
⊕ ⊖ ♁ Earth
♂ 1. Mars 2. Tuesday
♃ 1. Jupiter 2. Thursday
♄ 1. Saturn 2. Saturday
♅ ⛢ Uranus
♆ Neptune
♇ Pluto
✱ ✸ Star
☄ Comet
① ② ③ ④ Asteroids in chronological order of discovery

Signs of the Zodiac

Spring Signs
- ♈ Aries, the Ram
- ♉ Taurus, the Bull
- ♊ Ⅱ Gemini, the Twins

Summer Signs
- ♋ Cancer, the Crab
- ♌ Leo, the Lion
- ♍ Virgo, the Virgin

Autumn Signs
- ♎ Libra, the Balance
- ♏ Scorpio, the Scorpion
- ♐ Sagittarius, the Archer

Winter Signs
- ♑ ♑ Capricorn, the Goat
- ♒ Aquarius, the Water Bearer
- ♓ Pisces, the Fish

Aspects and Nodes

- ☌ conjunction; having the same longitude or right ascension

- ✻ sextile; differing by 60° in longitude or right ascension

▢ quadrature; differing by 90° in longitude **or**
    right ascension

△ trine; differing by 120° in longitude **or**
    right ascension

☍ opposition; differing by 180° in longitude **or**
    right ascension

☊ ascending node

☋ descending node

Notation Signs

β celestial latitude

Δ distance from Earth

δ declination

θ equation of light

λ longitude

μ proper motion

π parallax

ρ density

$\wp$ mean density

° degree(s) of arc

′ minute(s) of arc

″ second(s) of arc
+ North
− South

BIOLOGY

♂ 1. male organism or cell 2. staminate plant or flower
♀ 1. female organism or cell 2. pistillate plant or flower
○,⊙ annual plant
⊙⊙ biennial plant
♃ perennial herb or plant
⊙ monocarpic plant
△ evergreen plant
✕ crossed with: denoting a hybrid
∞ numerous or indefinite in number.
✳ northern hemisphere
✳̄ southern hemisphere
|✳ Old World
✳| New World

MEDICINE

- * birth
- † death
- □, ♂ male
- O, ♀ female
- + 1. excess of   2. acid reaction   3. positive reaction
- − 1. deficiency of   2. alkaline reaction 3. negative reaction
- Ⓐ admitted
- Ⓛ left
- Ⓡ right
- ⓜ heart murmur

MATHEMATICS

- + 1. plus, addition sign'   2. positive
- − 1. minus, subtraction sign   2. negative
- × times, multiplication sign
- ÷ divided by, division sign; division also indicated by an oblique line (8/2) or a horizontal line between dividend and divisor ($\frac{8}{2}$)

$=$	equals; is equal to
$\neq$	is not equal to
$\equiv$	is identical with; is congruent to; is equivalent to
$\approx$	is approximately equal to
$>$	is greater than
$<$	is less than
$\not>$	is not greater than
$\not<$	is not less than
$\cong$	is isomorphic to
$:$	is to; ratio sign
$::$	as: used between ratios
∞	infinity
$\therefore$	therefore
$\because$	since; because
$\angle$	angle
$\llcorner$	right angle
$\perp$	is perpendicular to
$\parallel$	is parallel to
$\bigcirc$	circle; circumference
$\frown$	arc of a circle
$\triangle$	triangle

□	square
▭	rectangle
▱	parallelogram
$\sqrt{}$	radical sign (*i.e.* square root sign)
Σ	sum
$\int$	integral
$\cup$	union
$\cap$	intersection
$\in$	is a member of; is an element of; belongs to
$\subset, \subseteq$	is a subset of
{ }	set braces
ϕ	the empty set
$\|\ \|$	absolute value of; modulus of
$\triangleleft$	is a normal subgroup of
μ	mean (population)
σ	standard deviation (population)
$\bar{x}$	mean (sample)
s	standard deviation (sample)
π	ratio of circumference of any circle to its diameter
e	base of natural logarithms

MISCELLANEOUS

    & ampersand
  &c. et cetera
   © copyright
   ′ foot, feet; minutes
  ″ inch(es); seconds
  × by: used in quoting dimensions
  < derived from: used in etymology
  ® registered trademark
  ¶ paragraph mark
  § section mark
  ″ ditto
  ° degree(s)

MUSIC

Time values of notes and rests
(Each note has half the value of the preceding note; the note symbol is followed by the equivalent rest symbol.)

‖◖‖, breve (rarely used)

o ▬ semibreve or whole note

♩ ▬ minim or half note

♩ ⸗ or ⸮ crotchet or quarter-note

♪ ⸯ quaver or eighth-note

♪ ⸱ semiquaver or
sixteenth-note

♪ ⸱ demisemiquaver or
thirty-second note

♪ ⸱ hemidemisemiquaver or
sixty-fourth note

NB: A dot after a note increases its value by a half.

Clefs in common use (with position of middle C shown)

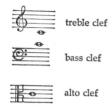

treble clef

bass clef

alto clef

Accidentals (*i.e.* signs indicating sharpening or flattening of notes)

♯   sharp – raise note one semitone

𝄪   double sharp – raise note one tone

♭   flat – lower note one semitone

♭♭   double flat – lower note one tone

♮   natural – after sharp or flat sign, restore note to normal pitch

Curved Lines

tie or bind; the two notes are played as one

slur or legato; play smoothly (in one bow on string instrument)

A curved line linking longer passages usually indicates phrasing.

Staccato marks and signs of accentuation

mezzo-staccato: shorten note by about ¼

staccato: shorten note by about ½

staccatissimo: shorten note by about ¾

detached: accented

attack

Ornaments and decorations

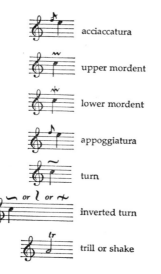

acciaccatura

upper mordent

lower mordent

appoggiatura

turn

inverted turn

trill or shake

Dynamics

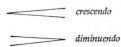

crescendo

diminuendo

Miscellaneous

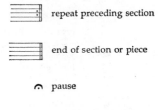

repeat preceding section

end of section or piece

pause

8ᵉ   play an octave above notes written